Charlotte Davies has years of experience both representing patients at Mental Health Tribunal hearings, and then sitting as a judge on the tribunal panel. She was called to the bar in 2007, having read law at Bristol University followed by an LLM at King's College London, with a focus on mental health law. After practising in London for three years, Charlotte moved to Cornwall with her young family and joined KBG Chambers, where she has a broad civil and general common law practice. In 2020, Charlotte was appointed as a Fee Paid First-Tier Tribunal Judge, sitting in the Health, Education and Social Care Chamber, and deployed to the Mental Health Tribunal. She is also a Deputy District Judge on the Western Circuit.

Charlotte has two young children, as well as five stepchildren, and lives with her husband, a retired police officer, in Truro, Cornwall.

A Practical Guide to the Mental Health Tribunal

A Practical Guide to the Mental Health Tribunal

Charlotte Davies
Barrister
LLB (Hons) LLM (London)
Deputy District Judge
Fee Paid Judge of the First-Tier Tribunal

Law Brief Publishing

Published 2023 by Law Brief Publishing, an imprint of Law Brief Publishing Ltd
30 The Parks
Minehead
Somerset
TA24 8BT

www.lawbriefpublishing.com

Paperback: 978-1-916698-12-3

PREFACE

The powers conferred by the Mental Health Act 1983, and the impact that the use of those powers can have on the lives of ordinary people and their families, is arguably incomparable to that of any other statute.

The removal of a citizen's liberty is something most of us would understand to be reserved for those that have committed terrible crimes. A punishment imposed by society for wrongdoing that cannot adequately be met by a lesser sanction. To remove a person's liberty, in order to mitigate risks associated with an illness, is an extraordinarily arbitrary course of action. As such, it is a power that requires rigorous checks and balances. Mental disorders and their associated symptoms are of course entirely outside a person's control, but there are occasions where the presentation is such that the use of the Mental Health Act 1983 can, quite literally, save lives. With that in mind, the Mental Health Tribunal (or the Mental Health Review Tribunal in Wales) is the body tasked with acting as that independent 'check and balance'.

This book aims to provide those who practise in the rewarding area of representing patients at Mental Health Tribunal hearings with an accessible and practical overview of what to expect both in the lead up to and during the hearing, with a necessary focus on the appeal hearing itself. Due to the very private nature of Mental Health Tribunal hearings, many representatives go into their first hearing without having had any specific training, and often without ever having even sat in on one at all. They have no idea what to expect, which, for a conscientious legal practitioner, can be extraordinarily stressful.

It is suggested that this book be read in conjunction with a more in-depth legal textbook, if the reader requires a more academic analysis. This book is designed to keep legalese to a minimum and references to case law to the absolutely essential. It has been set out with headings and sub-headings to enable you to pick it up and go straight to the topic that you need some fast and practical guidance on. Each chapter contains helpful summary bullet points at the end which highlight the key learning points within each section.

As of the date of publication, there is a Mental Health Bill being debated in Parliament. There is a short summary of the proposed key changes at the end of this book. This is the only reference to the Bill throughout the book, as the purpose is to set out the law and procedure as it is now. Equally, it is not certain what the final changes will look like and until Royal Assent is given, a detailed discussion of how things might change risks being speculative, at best.

The content of this book is correct as of 1 August 2023.

Charlotte Davies
August 2023

CONTENTS

RESOURCES

It is recommended that practitioners have access to and are familiar with the following (depending on jurisdiction), which are readily available online:

Mental Health Act 1983

Mental Health Act 1983: Code of Practice

Mental Health Act 1983: Code of Practice for Wales

Tribunal Procedure (First-Tier Tribunal) (Health, Education and Social Care Chamber) Rules 2008

Mental Health Review Tribunal for Wales Rules 2008

Tribunal Procedure (Upper Tribunal) Rules 2008

Practice Direction: First-Tier Tribunal: Health, Education and Social Care Chamber: Statements and Reports in Mental Health Cases 2013

The Law Society Practice Note: Representation before Mental Health Tribunals 2022

USEFUL ABBREVIATIONS

AC	Approved Clinician
AMHP	Approved Mental Health Practitioner
AWOL	Absent Without Leave
CAMHS	Child and Adolescent Mental Health Services
CC/CCo	Care Coordinator
CMHT	Community Mental Health Team
CPA meeting	Care Programme Approach meeting
CQC	Care Quality Commission
CTO	Community Treatment Order
DHSC	Department of Health and Social Care
DoLS	Deprivation of Liberty Safeguards
DSM	Diagnostic and Statistical Manual
ECHR	European Convention on Human Rights
ESR	Extra-Statutory Recommendation
FTT	First-Tier Tribunal
HESC	Health, Education and Social Care Chamber

HMH/HMR	Hospital Managers' Hearing or Hospital Managers' Review
HRA	Human Rights Act 1998
IMHA	Independent Mental Health Practitioner
LA	Local Authority
LAA	Legal Aid Agency
LPA	Lasting Power of Attorney
LASSA	Local Authority Social Services Authority
MAPPA	Multi-Agency Public Protection Arrangements
MARAC	Multi-Agency Risk Assessment Conference
MCA 2005	Mental Capacity Act 2005
MHA 1983	Mental Health Act 1983
MHAA	Mental Health Act Administrator
MHRT	Mental Health Review Tribunal (in Wales)
MHT	Mental Health Tribunal
MM	Medical Member
MoJ	Ministry of Justice
NICE	National Institute for Health and Care Excellence
NR	Nearest Relative

OT	Occupational Therapist
PHE	Pre-Hearing Examination
RA	Responsible Authority
RC	Responsible Clinician
SOAD	Second Opinion Appointed Doctor
SpLM	Specialist Lay Member
SRA	Solicitors Regulation Authority
UT	Upper Tribunal

CHAPTER ONE

WHAT IS THE MENTAL HEALTH TRIBUNAL?

Introduction

The Mental Health Tribunal (Mental Health Review Tribunal in Wales) is a branch of the Tribunals Service (which forms part of HMCTS: His Majesty's Courts and Tribunals Service), that sits within the Health, Education and Social Care Chamber.

All patients subject to 'sectioning' under the Mental Health Act 1983 have a right to appeal against that sectioning (save for those patients subject to short-term emergency powers, and those subject to interim orders or remand by the criminal court). Such right satisfies the requirements of the European Convention on Human Rights ('the ECHR') and the Human Rights Act 1998, in that it provides a fair hearing and a means to challenge any Article 8 interference (the right to respect for private and family life). The Mental Health Tribunal is entirely independent of the Responsible Authority (the body – usually an NHS Trust – which is exercising its powers under the Mental Health Act 1983 to detain a patient or make them liable to be detained, sometimes also referred to as the 'Detaining Authority').

These appeals are heard by a panel provided by the tribunal service. Appeals can arise via an application by the patient (or by the Nearest Relative), or via the process of automatic referrals (or 'references') by the hospital manager.

The term 'appeal' is used in its most basic sense: it is an appeal against the use of the Mental Health Act 1983 and not an appeal against a court order to a higher court. Therefore, a Mental Health Tribunal decision is a first instance decision.

The Mental Health Tribunal fulfils a judicial function and those attending a tribunal hearing should understand that they are attending what is essentially a court hearing. The apparent informal nature of a Mental Health Tribunal hearing can sometimes lead attendees, including professionals, to forget the judicial nature of the process. However, the informal nature of the hearing is solely for the benefit of the patient; to put them at ease and facilitate their participation. A legal professional will assist the panel far better when they keep its judicial function at the forefront of their mind. The burden of proof is on the Responsible Authority and the panel must weigh up the evidence and make findings of fact, on the balance of probabilities, and then apply the law to those facts. These core fundamentals should not be lost in the midst of the perceived informality of the process.

A Mental Health Tribunal three-person panel comprises a legally-trained judge (often a senior and experienced barrister or solicitor); a medical member, who will be a consultant psychiatrist (practising or retired); and a specialist member. The specialist member (sometimes referred to as the 'lay member', but undoubtedly more appropriately referred to as a 'specialist') can come from a variety of backgrounds, but predominately will have a social care background.

The Tribunal Rules stipulate that hearings are to be held in private, unless ordered otherwise and that it is in the patient's interests or the interests of justice for it to be held in public. This is due to the highly private and confidential nature of the patient's medical information being discussed, and it is this that makes it so difficult for legal practitioners to gain any real insight into the hearing process.

Appointment & Training

Appointments to the Mental Health Tribunal are made by the Judicial Appointments Commission (JAC), which is an independent body set up in 2006 under the terms of the Constitutional Reform Act 2005. It advertises judicial vacancies, receives applications, and then assesses applicants against a series of 'competencies': the ability to assimilate and clarify information; to work with others; to exercise judgement; to possess and build knowledge; to manage work efficiently; and to communicate effectively.

The process to become a Mental Health Tribunal judge is the same process through which court judges are appointed. It is a long and arduous year-long process which involves a written application, online exams, references, and a 'selection day' which includes role plays and an interview. At present, applicants cannot specifically elect to be appointed to the Mental Health Tribunal but are asked to rank their order of preference between the various tribunals (which include Immigration & Asylum, Tax, and Social Entitlement). Successful applicants are then notified of the chamber and jurisdiction to which they will be deployed.

The majority of Mental Health Tribunal judges sit part time as 'fee-paid' members and are paid a daily fee rather than a full-time salary. There is a group of full-time salaried Mental Health Tribunal judges in England who are appointed from the fee-paid ranks and take on more senior responsibilities.

Medical members and specialist members are also appointed by the JAC through similar processes.

Training is provided by the Judicial College and includes initial intensive on-boarding, followed by yearly minimum training updates. All panel members are also regularly appraised.

Jurisdiction

The Mental Health Tribunal's powers derive from the Mental Health Act 1959 which established the Mental Health Review Tribunal. Subsequent amendments were made by the Mental Health Acts 1983 and 2007.

In England, the tribunal is now referred to as the Mental Health Tribunal, but it remains as the Mental Health Review Tribunal in Wales. The Health, Education and Social Care Chamber does not encompass the Welsh Mental Health Review Tribunal, which operates via s.65 of the Mental Health Act 1983. The Welsh tribunal's procedure is governed by the Mental Health Review Tribunal for Wales Rules 2008. The Tribunal Procedure (First-Tier Tribunal) (Health, Education and Social Care Chamber) Rules 2008 govern the English Mental Health Tribunal.

Prior to the Tribunals, Courts and Enforcement Act 2007, the only means to challenge a decision of the Mental Health Tribunal was by way of judicial review. Since the 2007 Act, a tribunal judge can set aside a decision if there is a clear error of law, and can grant permission to appeal to the Upper Tribunal. The Upper Tribunal hears appeals from both the Mental Health Tribunal and the Mental Health Review Tribunal.

The inquisitorial nature of the Mental Health Tribunal

Whilst the function of the Mental Health Tribunal is judicial in nature, proceedings are generally 'inquisitorial' as opposed to 'adversarial'. In court proceedings, the process is adversarial with two (or more) opposed sides, often legally represented, setting out their respective cases and the judge applying strict rules of evidence and procedure throughout. Sanctions can be as severe as having an entire claim struck out for lack of compliance with those rules or for breaches of previous court orders. In an 'inquisitorial' hearing, the panel can be more proactive in asking questions and apply a greater degree of flexibility to managing the process. The Mental Health Tribunal will go well out of its way to afford the patient a fair hearing. Legal representatives who are used to appearing in court and who might not have encountered an inquisitorial process before, should adapt their approach accordingly. A combative approach will not be well received by a tribunal panel, and almost certainly would not be in the best interests of the patient.

As well as a non-combative approach, the inquisitorial nature of the Mental Health Tribunal means that the strict rules of evidence do not apply as they would in court. The patient does not need to provide any form of pre-disclosed written statement; they can say what they like on the day. Evidence before the tribunal is often, by its very nature, full of hearsay (taken from previous records, notes and other professionals' reports), and fresh information can be sprung on a legal representative mid-hearing in a manner that a court-seasoned practitioner might describe as being 'ambushed'. Tribunals can take short breaks to enable a witness to go and find something out, if deemed necessary. Legal practitioners must learn very quickly that a Mental Health Tribunal hearing is far more collaborative than it is combative.

The Code of Practice & the Guiding Principles

Section 18 of the Mental Health Act 1983 requires the Secretary of State (and Welsh equivalent) to establish a Code of Practice which must embody a set of 'guiding principles'. It is vital for any legal practitioner working in the area of mental health law to be familiar with both the Code and the guiding principles, which are set out as follows:

- ***Least restrictive option and maximising independence*** where it is possible to treat a patient safely and lawfully without detaining them under the Act, the patient should not be detained. Wherever possible a patient's independence should be encouraged and supported with a focus on promoting recovery.

- *Empowerment and involvement* patients should be fully involved in decisions about care, support and treatment. The views of families, carers and others, if appropriate, should be fully considered when taking decisions. Where decisions are taken which are contradictory to views expressed, professionals should explain the reasons for this.

- *Respect and dignity* patients, their families and carers should be treated with respect and dignity and listened to by professionals.

- *Purpose and effectiveness* decisions about care and treatment should be appropriate to the patient, with clear therapeutic aims, promote recovery and should be performed to current national guidelines and/or current available best practice guidelines.

- *Efficiency and equity* providers, commissioners and other relevant organisations should work together to ensure that the quality of commissioning and provision of mental healthcare services are of high quality and are given equal priority to physical health and social care services. All relevant services should work together to facilitate timely, safe and supportive discharge from detention.

The Code of Practice applies to medical practitioners, approved clinicians, hospital managers and hospital staff in relation to the admission of patients to hospital, as well as to Guardianship and Community Treatment Orders. It applies to doctors and other professionals providing medical treatment to patients suffering from a mental disorder, as well as to patients who are in hospital informally, or indeed not in hospital at all.

SUMMARY

- The Mental Health Tribunal acts as an independent 'check and balance' on the powers arising out of the Mental Health Act 1983.
- Almost all patients subject to the powers of the Act are entitled to appeal against their section.
- The Judicial Appointments Commission is in charge of appointing those who sit on the Mental Health Tribunal panels.
- The Mental Health Tribunal's jurisdiction derives from the Mental Health Act 1959 (as amended), and the Tribunal's procedure is governed by the Tribunal Procedure (First-Tier Tribunal) (Health, Education and Social Care Chamber) Rules 2008, and Welsh equivalent.
- The process is inquisitorial rather than adversarial.
- The Upper Tribunal hears appeals from the Mental Health Tribunal and the Mental Health Review Tribunal in Wales.
- The Code of Practice and guiding principles are essential reading for all practitioners in mental health law.

CHAPTER TWO

THE MENTAL HEALTH TRIBUNAL'S POWERS

Introduction

The Mental Health Tribunal's powers are set out in sections 72 to 75 of the Mental Health Act 1983. These encompass the power (and duty) to discharge a patient (as well as to defer that discharge), and to make both formal and informal recommendations. The Mental Health Tribunal also has case management powers which are vital in overseeing and properly progressing a patient's application or reference.

If a panel is not satisfied that the statutory criteria applicable to the particular patient are met, then the tribunal *must* discharge. The burden of proof rests with the Responsible Authority to demonstrate that the criteria for detention are met, and the standard of proof is the civil standard (**R(N) v Mental Health Review Tribunal (Northern Region) [2005]**): on the balance of probabilities, meaning that it is more likely that not that a particular aspect of the criteria has been met, following the factual findings that have been made. Strictly, the patient does not have to prove anything.

Deferred discharge: s.72(3)

If a panel defers discharge under s.72(3) (which can only be done to allow time to make arrangements), then it must specify a date for that discharge, and the discharge will take place on that specific date even if the patient's circumstances have subsequently changed. Deferred discharge cannot be used to test the patient's readiness for discharge (**Central & North West London NHS Foundation Trust v H-JH**

[2012]). It is this that makes panels extremely reluctant to direct a deferred discharge, and legal representatives should have this in mind when considering such an application. If it is an application that does feel appropriate to a legal representative, then clear evidence is going to be needed that all arrangements that need to be put in place will be in place by the deferral date. Any lack of or uncertainty in the evidence regarding post-discharge arrangements should be dealt with by consideration of an adjournment, and not by way of a deferred discharge (**R(H) v Ashworth Hospital Authority** [2002]).

Discretionary powers: s.72(1)

Use of the Mental Health Tribunal's discretionary powers to discharge apply solely to non-restricted patients, and even then, in exceptional circumstances only. If a panel is not satisfied that the criteria for detention are met then it must discharge the patient. If it is satisfied, then it will not. It is difficult to imagine therefore in what circumstances a panel will determine that the criteria are met but then exercise its discretion to discharge. Nonetheless, many legal representatives make the submission that this is exactly what a panel should do, but such a submission rarely succeeds. One example might be discretionary discharge to receive treatment in the patient's home country.

Case Management

It is vital that the Mental Health Tribunal has the ability to effectively manage an appeal through to its conclusion at the hearing. In doing so, the matter must be handled with fairness and in the interests of justice. The 'overriding objective' of dealing with cases justly and proportionately will the principle that overarches all case management decisions. The Tribunal Procedure Rules therefore provide wide-ranging case management powers to, for example, direct the filing of certain reports or documents; postpone the hearing if necessary; adjourn the hearing on the day; appoint legal representatives under Rule 11(7)(a) or Rule

11(7)(b); summons witnesses, and give consent to the withdrawal of an application.

Case management is undertaken both in the lead up to the hearing and also during the hearing itself. Applications to postpone a hearing, for example, are dealt with by the Tribunal Office. If the Tribunal Office is notified that any of the required reports have not been filed, then it can send out a directions order stipulating a date by which this needs to be done. Unlike in the courts however, the Mental Health Tribunal would not 'strike out' an application, or the Responsible Authority's right to present its case, because of a lack of compliance with a direction. However, it can, for example, summons a Chief Executive of an NHS Trust to come and explain themselves before the panel if a breach is so serious that it has caused prejudicial delay to a patient's right to a fair hearing. As one might imagine, an NHS Trust would likely be keen to avoid this.

How applications to withdraw and adjourn are dealt with during a hearing is dealt with in a later section.

Recommendations: s.72(3) & (3A)

The Mental Health Tribunal has the power to make both statutory and informal recommendations. Statutory recommendations can only be made with a view to facilitating discharge at some later date, and are limited to matters regarding s.17 leave, transfer to a different hospital, and transfer into Guardianship. The Mental Health Tribunal can also recommend that the Responsible Clinician consider the making of a Community Treatment Order. The panel cannot recommend that a patient be discharged onto a Community Treatment Order, only that it be considered. Although statutory recommendations do not legally compel the Responsible Authority to act, if it fails to do so then the Mental Health Tribunal can reconvene the panel and put pressure on the Responsible Authority to comply.

For a legal representative considering making such an application, it is worth noting that a panel should not make a recommendation where there is evidence that the treating team has given or is giving ongoing thought to the issue. In those circumstances, a recommendation would add nothing to the situation (**RB v Nottinghamshire Healthcare NHS Trust** [2011]).

Panels are often asked to, and indeed can of its own volition, make observations or comments in the decision, which are not legally binding but could be viewed as an informal recommendation. The Mental Health Tribunal has no jurisdiction over the patient's treatment but a panel might sometimes consider the persuasive value of comments about activities the patient has expressed a particular desire to participate in but that the ward has not yet facilitated, or, for example, that the team undertake some different investigations or assessments. Legal representatives are often asked by patients to push for certain things at the hearing. For example, if a patient says that they have not been able to access a telephone to call a particular friend or family member, it should be explained to the patient that although the panel can certainly be asked to comment on the request, they would not be able to compel the treating team to act.

It is worth bearing in mind that the tribunal hearing might be the first opportunity that the patient has had to express their wishes and wants, at least to anybody outside of their treating team, and the value of this to the patient should not be underestimated.

Powers in Community Treatment Order (CTO) and Guardianship cases

The powers of the Mental Health Tribunal in respect of CTO and Guardianship cases are broadly the same as with other patients, but as a patient subject to a CTO is no longer in hospital then there are no statutory recommendations that could be made with a view to facilitating discharge. The Mental Health Tribunal does not have any jurisdiction over the conditions attached to a CTO.

It is important to note that in Guardianship cases, the burden of proof rests with the patient to show that the criteria are not met.

Restricted patients: s.37/41

Section 73 of the Mental Health Act 1983 deals with restricted patients and the powers of the Mental Health Tribunal. The consent of the Secretary of State is required in order to discharge a restricted patient and the Mental Health Tribunal's discretionary powers are not applicable to restricted patients. Restricted patients can also be discharged by the Secretary of State (s.42).

Although restricted patients can be discharged absolutely, this happens rarely given the reason for detention is the committing of a criminal offence, as well as the very fact of the imposition of the restriction order in the first place. It is far more likely that a conditional discharge will occur. This is where very strict conditions are placed on a patient such that they can be discharged from hospital as safely as possible. The Secretary of State reserves the power to recall the patient back to hospital and there is no legal threshold for doing so (however the Codes of Practice identify factors for consideration, with the safety of the public being at the forefront). This is a highly complex area that has resulted in a number of legal challenges. The most important principle is that whilst the law places no limit on the amount or type of conditions imposed, no condition can amount to a deprivation of the patient's liberty (**Secretary of State for Justice v MM [2018]**).

Patients can apply to the Mental Health Tribunal after 12 months of the conditional discharge (s.75). The Mental Health Tribunal can grant an absolute discharge, or can vary the conditions imposed. Note the disparity with the Mental Health Tribunal's powers, or lack thereof, regarding CTO conditions. One might have expected the Mental Health

Tribunal to have fewer powers over restricted patient conditions. Furthermore, it is for the patient to prove on a balance of probabilities that the necessity for the conditions no longer exists.

Unlike unrestricted patients, if the panel directs a deferred conditional discharge under s.73(7), it cannot specify a date and it does not necessarily mean that the patient will be discharged. If the necessary arrangements cannot be made, then the decision can be reversed. As with unrestricted patients, the panel cannot defer discharge to test the patient or gather further information. There is no power to defer an absolute discharge.

In the case of restricted patients, the Mental Health Tribunal has no power to make statutory recommendations. However, an 'extra-statutory recommendation' is something that a legal representative can ask for by arguing that additional s.17 leave, for example, is part of the 'appropriate treatment' criterion. This is not binding and, in reality, amounts to no more than an informal recommendation or comment.

SUMMARY

- The tribunal's powers are set out in sections 72 to 75 of the Act.
- The tribunal has important and wide-ranging case management powers.
- The 'overriding objective' is the overarching principle that will guide all case management decisions.
- If the criteria are not met, the panel must discharge the patient from their section.

- In most cases the burden of proof is on the Responsible Authority to demonstrate, on a balance of probabilities, that the criteria are met.

- The tribunal has the power to make statutory and informal recommendations.

- The consent of the Secretary of State is needed to discharge restricted patients.

CHAPTER THREE

SECTIONING UNDER THE MENTAL HEALTH ACT 1983

Introduction

It is useful for a legal representative acting for a patient subject to the powers of the Mental Health Act 1983, to understand exactly how their client came to be subject to those powers. As with any form of effective advocacy, there must be an underlying knowledge of the reasons and basis upon which the client has found themselves in the position that they are in. Not only that, such knowledge is vital in order to understand how the Responsible Authority will likely present its evidence, given the legal thresholds and chronology of the patient's involvement with mental health services leading up to an admission under the Act.

This chapter is designed to give a relatively brief overview of the legal requirements for sectioning under the Mental Health Act 1983 to provide a foundational level of understanding that can be built upon with additional reading if so desired.

'Civil' patients

Part II of the Mental Health Act 1983 deals with patients who are admitted to hospital via the 'civil' route: by mental health professionals, instead of through the criminal justice system. The relevant part of the Code of Practice is Chapter 14 (Chapter 5 in Wales). The following sections deal with how the various 'civil' parts of the Act are used.

Admission for Assessment: Section 2

Section 2 of the Mental Health Act 1983 provides for compulsory admission to hospital for assessment for a period of 28 days. Section 2 will be used for patients who have been admitted to hospital for the first time. The s.2 period cannot be renewed (save for under section 29(4) where court proceedings have been brought to displace a Nearest Relative). During the 28-day period, the s.2 can be regraded to a s.3 (admission for treatment).

To be detained under s.2, a patient must be suffering from a mental disorder of a nature or degree which warrants detention in hospital for assessment, or assessment followed by treatment, for at least a limited period; and, the patient ought to be detained in the interests of their own health or safety, or for the protection of others.

The application to admit a patient to hospital under the Act is made by an Approved Mental Health Practitioner (AMHP), or by the Nearest Relative. It is a matter of judgement by the AMHP as to whether or not an application is made. The application is made based on recommendations from two registered medical practitioners and there are standard forms on which this should be done.

Admission for Treatment: Section 3

Where a patient has had involvement with mental health services before, and has a diagnosis of a mental disorder, then section 3 is likely to be used.

Under s.3, patients are admitted to hospital for treatment for a period of up to six months. Unlike the s.2 28-day period, the s.3 six-month period can be renewed.

To be detained under s.3, a patient must be suffering from a mental disorder of a nature or degree which makes it appropriate for them to receive medical treatment in hospital; and, it is necessary for the health or safety of the patient, or for the protection of others, that the patient should receive such treatment, and that treatment cannot be provided unless the patient is detained; and, appropriate treatment is available.

As with applications under s.2, an application to detain a patient under s.3 is made by an AMHP, or a Nearest Relative, based on the recommendations of two registered medical practitioners, using the relevant proforma.

Section 4: Emergency Powers

Section 4 of the Mental Health Act 1983 grants emergency powers that enable the detention of a patient for no more than 72 hours, where compliance with the provisions of s.2 would cause 'undesirable delay' (s.4(2)). An emergency would be an immediate and significant risk of harm to the patient or others; danger of serious harm to property; or a need to physically restrain the patient (Code of Practice, Chapter 5.6).

An AMHP or the Nearest Relative can apply in cases where there is 'urgent necessity' (s.4(1)). Only one medical recommendation is required and the clinician must certify that obtaining a second recommendation would cause undesirable delay. If the second recommendation is obtained within the 72-hour period, then the s.4 can be converted into a s.2 admission.

Section 5: Holding Powers

Section 5 grants powers to detain a patient already in hospital voluntarily and can be used in any setting, including in any ward in a general hospital. Certain practitioners or clinicians can provide a report to the hospital manager stating that an application for compulsory detention should be made, and the effect of that report is that the patient can be detained for up to 72 hours. A Level 1 or 2 nurse with a practice in mental health or learning disability can, in writing, state that it is not practicable to obtain the attendance of a relevant practitioner or clinician, which allows the patient to be detained for up to six hours. The holding power does not allow treatment without the patient's consent.

Guardianship

Guardianship is dealt with in sections 7 to 10 of the Mental Health Act 1983, and Chapter 30 of the Code of Practice (Chapter 6 in Wales). It does not involve an admission into hospital and does not deprive a patient of their liberty.

Guardianship can be used if the patient is suffering from a mental disorder of a nature or degree which warrants reception into Guardianship (s.7(2)(a)), and it is necessary in the interests of the welfare of the patient or for the protection of others that they are received into Guardianship (s.7(2)(b)).

Guardianship gives the guardian (usually the local authority) power to require that the patient resides at a specified place; that they attend at a certain time and place for treatment, occupation education or training; and the power to require that access be given to any medical practitioner, AMHP or any other specified person (s.8(1)).

Community Treatment Orders: Section 17A

Brought in by the Mental Health Act 2007, Community Treatment Orders (CTOs) create a legal framework for treating patients in the community. Chapter 29 of the Code of Practice deals with CTOs and describes their purpose as "*...to provide a way to help prevent relapse and any harm...*" and states that they are "*...intended to help patients to maintain stable mental health outside hospital and promote recovery*".

The Responsible Clinician, with agreement of the AMHP, can discharge a patient onto a CTO if the patient is suffering from a mental disorder of a nature or degree which makes it appropriate that they should receive medical treatment; it is necessary for the patient's health or safety or for the protection of others that they should receive treatment; the treatment can be provided outside of hospital; it is necessary that the Responsible Clinician be able to exercise the power of recall to hospital; and appropriate treatment is available. A patient detained under s.2 cannot be made subject to a CTO.

The initial period of a CTO is six months. This can be renewed for a further six months, and then subsequently for periods of one year.

The Responsible Clinician can exercise the power of recall if in their view the patient requires medical treatment in hospital for their mental disorder, and there would be a risk of harm to their health or safety or to others if the patient was not recalled. The existence of the CTO means that the threshold for admission to hospital is lower than it is for detention under s.2 or s.3. If the patient is recalled to hospital, then they are treated as if they are detained under s.3, and a referral must be made to the Mental Health Tribunal. The criteria to be applied by the panel at the hearing will be the s.3 criteria.

Patients sectioned via the Criminal Justice System

Part III of the Mental Health Act 1983 deals with the admission to hospital and treatment of patients from the criminal justice system.

Part III patients can be both restricted and unrestricted. A court can sentence a person to a hospital order under s.37 without restrictions, and such patients would be treated as s.3 patients, save that they cannot apply to the Mental Health Tribunal during the first six months. Hospital orders are imposed where a patient has committed a crime but is deemed not to have had the capacity to form the intent to have committed that crime.

If a restriction order is made under s.41 and s.45A of the Act, the Responsible Clinician will not be able to discharge the patient. The Secretary of State retains the decision on leave, transfer, and discharge. Restricted patients do not have a Nearest Relative.

Section 17 leave

A lot will be said about 's.17 leave' within the statutory reports and during the tribunal hearing, and so it is worth a legal representative having a full understanding of what this is. It is a vital part of the process of working towards a discharge from the patient's section and crucial to testing any risk factors that the treating team might be concerned about. Therefore, it is important for the legal representative to review the patient's notes and ascertain whether or not the patient has been 'written up' for leave and how this has gone.

Section 17 allows patients who are subject to certain sections of the Act to be granted leave of absence. It also applies (but with modifications) to those patients who are subject to a restriction order. Leave cannot be granted to patients subject to s.5, CTO recall, remanded to hospital under s.35 or s.36, detained in hospital as a place of safety, or subject to an interim hospital order under s.38.

Leave will often be described as 'ground leave' if it is limited to the hospital grounds, and be either 'escorted' or 'unescorted'. To begin with it can be limited to periods of 30 minutes or less. Often, the aim will be to increase leave to overnight leave back to the patient's community accommodation, and patients can sometimes be placed on 'extended s.17 leave'.

Section 117 aftercare

Section 117 of the Act places a duty on the Clinical Commissioning Group (CCG) and the local authority to provide aftercare services to certain patients following their discharge from section. There is no charge to the patient for s.117 aftercare. Which CCG and local authority are responsible for the s.117 aftercare will be determined by where the patient was resident prior to their detention.

Patients who have been detained under sections 3, 37, 45A, 47 or 48 are eligible for s.117 aftercare. Aftercare lasts as long as there is a need to be met, and extends to accommodation if a specialist placement is needed.

The patient's eligibility for s.117 aftercare is important because it can determine the likelihood of any risks being managed in the community.

SUMMARY

- Legal representatives should have a good understanding of how patients come to be subject to the Mental Health Act 1983.
- Section 2 of the Act provides for compulsory admission to hospital for assessment for a period of 28 days. The section cannot be renewed but can be regraded to s.3.
- Under section 3 of the Act, patients are admitted to hospital for treatment for a period of up to six months. The section can be renewed.
- Applications to detain a patient under s.2 or s.3 are made by an AMHP, or a Nearest Relative, based on the recommendations of two registered medical practitioners, using the relevant proforma.
- The Act also grants emergency and holding powers.

- Community Treatment Orders create a legal framework for patients to be treated in the community whilst subject to a power of recall. The Responsible Clinician's power to recall the patient to hospital must be necessary and not just desirable.

- Patients who are admitted to hospital from the criminal justice system can be both restricted and unrestricted. If a patient is restricted, then the Responsible Clinician cannot discharge them.

- S.17 leave is an important part of the process of working towards discharge.

- Free s.117 aftercare is available to patients who have been detained on longer-term sections and then discharged from hospital.

CHAPTER FOUR

WHEN DOES A MENTAL HEALTH TRIBUNAL HEARING HAPPEN?

Introduction

Part V of the Mental Health Act 1983 sets out the rights of patients to apply to the Mental Health Tribunal, and the duties on hospital managers to make a referral on the patient's behalf. The following sections deal with 'civil' patients subject to Part II of the Mental Health Act 1983. Patients subject to the criminal procedure under Part III are discussed at the end of the chapter.

The application and reference processes are unaffected by each other. There is nothing preventing a patient applying immediately following a hearing of an automatic reference and so it is not unusual to have Mental Health Tribunal hearings in quick succession. If this situation arises, a legal representative should carefully consider the timeline and the patient's prospects of success at the hearing, and weigh up if it might be worth withdrawing the application until a later date, so as to maximise the patient's prospects of discharge.

Applications

An application to the Mental Health Tribunal must be made within the first 14 days if the patient is detained under s.2. If the deadline is missed, then the Secretary of State can be asked to made a referral to the Mental Health Tribunal.

If the patient is detained under s.3, then an application can be made within the first six-month period, within the second six-month period, and then annually following that; effectively, within any subsequent renewal period.

For a patient subject to a Community Treatment Order, the patient can apply within the first six-month period from the day the CTO was made, and then within any further periods of renewal. Again, once within any renewal period.

If a patient changes sections, so for example they were subject to s.3 and are then placed on a CTO, they can apply again. If, whilst awaiting a hearing following an application made during a s.2 detention, the patient is regraded to s.3, and the hearing then takes place; the panel will apply the s.3 criteria as that is the criteria under which the patient is detained on the day of the hearing. However, the patient will then be able to apply again as they will not have used their application rights for the s.3 period. Therefore, a patient can have two hearings within one period of detention but these are borne from applications arising out of the two separate periods.

Capacity Issues

If the patient lacks the capacity to make an application to the Mental Health Tribunal, then any application made is liable to be struck out. Given the Mental Health Tribunal process is crucial to the patient challenging the decision to detain, the threshold for capacity has been set very low. In **SM v Livewell Southwest [2020]** it was held that all the patient needs to understand is that they are being detained against their wishes, and the Mental Health Tribunal has the power to discharge them. There are a number of protections afforded to patients who are determined to lack capacity to bring a valid application: the Secretary of State can be asked to submit a reference to the Mental Health Tribunal, in addition to the automatic reference procedure as set out below.

References

In addition to the application process, hospital managers have a duty to refer a patient to the Mental Health Tribunal at various intervals depending on the patient's section. This provides a safeguard for patients who do not make use of their application rights and upholds the patient's Article 5 ECHR rights (the right to liberty and security).

If the patient is detained under s.2 or s.3, then a referral must be made on the expiry of six months from the date of admission to hospital, unless the patient has already applied to the Mental Health Tribunal. A reference is also made when a CTO is revoked. Long term patients detained under s.3 will be referred if they have not had a Mental Health Tribunal hearing for a period of three years. If the patient is under 18 then a reference will be made following a year during which their case has not been heard by a Mental Health Tribunal.

Discretionary References

The Secretary of State has a discretion to refer a patient's case to the Mental Health Tribunal under s.62 Mental Health Act 1983. Any person can make the request but such request must be supported by evidence setting out the reasons. There is government guidance available to assist with such applications.

Nearest Relative Applications

The role of Nearest Relative is very important and comes with a number of rights. Many Nearest Relatives are unaware of the powers that they hold in terms of sectioned patients. They can object to an application for admission under s.3 or to a Guardianship application under s.7; they can also compel discharge of patients detained pursuant to sections 2, 3 and 7, as well as those subject to a CTO.

The Responsible Clinician can bar an order for discharge by the Nearest Relative but if this is done in a s.3 or CTO case, the Nearest Relative can then apply to the Mental Health Tribunal for discharge. For patients detained under s.2, the Nearest Relative has no right to apply to the Mental Health Tribunal, although like any person they could make a request to the Secretary of State for a discretionary reference.

Mental Health Tribunal Applications for Part III Patients

The opportunity to come before a Mental Health Tribunal is more limited for Part III patients because their detention has arisen following a court order. Given this, such patients can only apply to the Mental Health Tribunal six months after the date of said order (patients detained pursuant to s.37, s.37/41, s.45A). Transferred patients can apply to the Mental Health Tribunal immediately (s.47 and s.48). Patients subject to a Guardianship order under s.37 can make an application within the first six months. Thereafter applications can be made within each renewal period. There is no access to the Mental Health Tribunal for patients subject to s.35 or s.36 shorter terms powers.

For patients subject to s.37, the Nearest Relative can make an application during each period of section for a hospital order, and in the first 12 months, then annually, for patients subject to a Guardianship order.

Restricted Patients

If the court considers that the public need to be protected from serious harm, it can also impose a restriction order under s.41 in addition to the s.37 hospital order. Section 41 restrictions mean that the Secretary of State must consent to certain aspects of the patient's management, such as hospital transfers and discharge into the community. Restricted patients do not have Nearest Relatives.

Insofar as references for restricted patients are concerned, the Secretary of State takes on a number of duties, along with a general discretion to make a referral to the Mental Health Tribunal at any time. A reference must be made when no hearing has taken place within the previous three years, and if a conditionally discharged patient is recalled to hospital, then the Secretary of State must make a reference within one month.

SUMMARY

- Mental Health Tribunal hearings can be convened in two ways: following an application, or as a result of an automatic referral. The two regimes work independently and are unaffected by each other.

- An application to the tribunal must be made within 14 days of the s.2 commencing.

- Applications can be made within each renewal period of a s.3 or a CTO.

- References must be made at certain intervals and as a result of certain events, for example, a CTO being revoked.

- The Secretary of State has a discretion to refer a patient to the Mental Health Tribunal and any person can make a request for this.

- The role of the Nearest Relative is very important and comes with a number of powers, including the power to compel discharge of the patient in certain cases. If this is barred by the Responsible Clinician, the Nearest Relative can then apply to the Mental Health Tribunal.

- Part III patients have more limited access to the Mental Health Tribunal with most patients having to wait six months before they can apply. There is also a regime of automatic references for restricted patients.

CHAPTER FIVE

MAKING AN APPLICATION

Introduction

This chapter will give an overview of the process involved in making an application to the Mental Health Tribunal to appeal a patient's section.

Throughout this process, it is important for a legal representative to keep the enormity of the situation for the patient at the forefront of their mind. The patient has been deprived of their liberty in a manner which they are likely to find very confusing and overwhelming. Their detention might have arisen from an extremely distressing and traumatic incident. It is therefore important that the patient understands, insofar as they are able, exactly what steps are being taken and why, as well as what is expected to happen next in the process, and when.

Taking Instructions and Advising

It is good practice to formulate a checklist of questions to ask the patient at the first meeting. Time will be limited and so obtaining the information needed to begin preparing the arguments that will be used at any subsequent hearing is going to be crucial. It is equally if not more important that the patient understands the legal representative's role, and the limits of that role. Building a rapport is essential for the patient to feel comfortable come the time of the hearing, which will facilitate them being able to give their best evidence to the panel. Rapport is also needed to instil trust and confidence. However, the legal representative's role is a professional one and that comes with the duty of confidentiality: nothing can be disclosed without the patient's instructions (if the patient discloses an intention to self-harm, or an intention to harm others, the legal representative may be permitted in law to disclose this information. The advice is to seek guidance from the SRA or other professional body).

Key questions to ask at the first meeting could include:

- Why were they brought into hospital?
- What happened in the immediate lead up to the admission?
- If they stopped taking their medication, when and why was this?
- Is illicit drug use an issue?
- Do they agree with the diagnosis?
- Have they been in hospital before?
- Have they had s.17 leave and if so, how is it going?
- Has the medication made them feel better?
- Have there been any difficulties on the ward such as arguments or physical altercations?
- What do they want the tribunal to do?
- If the panel discharged them, where would they go?
- Would they continue to take their medication if discharged?
- Would they engage with community mental health services?

There is a presumption in law that a person has capacity until proven otherwise (Mental Capacity Act 2005 s.1(2)), and the threshold for capacity is low. There is no need for the patient to be able to give detailed instructions on what are likely to be complex medical matters. If, however, a legal representative believes that the patient lacks capacity then they cannot be instructed to make an application to the Mental Health Tribunal. In such circumstances, there is power under s.67(1) Mental Health Act 1983 to ask the Secretary of State to refer the case to the Mental Health Tribunal.

In the case of non-restricted patients, a legal representative will need to ascertain who the Nearest Relative is and explain the powers that the Nearest Relative has to the patient. Instructions should be taken on whether or not the patient wants them to be contacted and whether it would be supportive to any application to the Mental Health Tribunal to have them involved. A patient has a right to say that they do not want the Nearest Relative involved.

A sensible legal representative will also review the section papers to ensure that the detention is lawful in the first instance.

The Application Procedure: Rule 32

Rule 32 of the Tribunal Procedure (First-Tier Tribunal) (Health, Education and Social Care Chamber) Rules 2008 sets out the procedure for making the application which must be in writing and signed, either by the patient or by a person authorised to do so on their behalf. There are standard forms available online. If the patient is detained under s.2, the patient has 14 days in which to make the application. The legal representative should ensure that any application is made in accordance with the eligibility periods of the section under which they are subject to.

The legal representative should copy the Mental Health Act Administrator into the email when filing the application with the Tribunal Office (filing by email is preferable). At the same time, signed authority from the patient should be sent to the Responsible Clinician giving permission to access the notes. A thorough analysis of the notes, once received, will be an important part of the preparation for the legal representative.

In all but s.2 cases, the Mental Health Act Administrator has three weeks from date of receipt in which to file the statutory reports with the Tribunal Office, on which date automatic directions should be sent out chasing these. Directions can be requested under Rule 5(d) if reports have not been filed within this timeframe, and the Responsible Authority chased directly.

A legal representative should consider whether a pre-hearing examination should be requested (such a request is required in all cases save for patients detained under s.2 in which it will take place automatically).

What happens next?

Upon receiving an application to appeal a section, or a reference, the Mental Health Tribunal will notify those who need to be aware. This is done by way of a CNL1 (Case Notification Letter) in all cases save for s.2 patients due to the short timescales involved. The CNL1 will identify a period in which the appeal will be heard (the 'listing window'). The parties will be invited to submit their dates of availability within that listing window (via a form called an HQ1) and will also be informed of the deadlines for the filing of reports. There is no CNL1 or equivalent in Wales.

In terms of timescales, a hearing within seven days should be expected for a patient detained under s.2; within two months if admitted for treatment; and within four months for restricted patients. The only timescales specified within the Rules are the seven days for s.2 patients, and that following the recall of a conditionally discharged patient the hearing must start no more than eight weeks after the reference.

Postponements

Applications to postpone a hearing due to unavailability of the legal representative (or an independent expert) will need to be made on form CMR1 and should be based on instructions from the patient. The application should make it clear that the patient has confirmed that they wish to be represented by the particular representative and the reasons for this, for example they have known the patient for many years. The application should also make clear that the patient understands that a postponement will result in a delay to the appeal being heard. It is important that the application sets out when all the parties will be available for a relisted hearing, and it is suggested that there be liaison with the Responsible Authority in this respect.

SUMMARY

- It is good practice to have a pre-prepared list of questions to ask the patient at the first meeting.
- It is important that the patient understands the role of the legal representative, including their duty of confidentiality.
- A patient must have capacity to be able to make an application to the tribunal. There is a low threshold for this.
- The legal representative should ensure that any application is made in accordance with the eligibility periods of the section under which the patient is subject.
- A patient has the right to say that they do not want the Nearest Relative involved in the process.

- Rule 32 sets out the procedure for applying to the tribunal. It is good practice to email the application to the MHAA at the same time as the Tribunal Office.

- The legal representative should send a signed authority to the Responsible Clinician for access to the patient's notes.

- Consideration should be given to requesting a PHE.

- Applications for a postponement should be made on form CMR1.

CHAPTER SIX

THE WRITTEN EVIDENCE

Introduction

It is from the written evidence that the panel will glean its first impressions of the patient. When a panel is appointed, the Tribunal Office will forward any reports and other documents it has on file to the panel members who will read these carefully prior to holding their pre-hearing discussion. It might be said that the Responsible Authority has the first opportunity to get its 'foot in the door' insofar as persuading the panel of the criteria being met. This is because the burden of proof is on the Responsible Authority, despite the patient bringing the appeal. The legal representative should therefore approach the reports with this in mind.

The Statutory Reports

The 'statutory reports' are a set of reports from the Responsible Authority which form a significant part of the evidence that the panel will consider. They are the springboard from which all the questions of the witnesses are asked.

The reports usually comprise a medical report, a nursing report and a social circumstances report. Often, addendums have to be filed if a hearing has been adjourned and the reports are then too out of date to be useful to the panel hearing the re-listed hearing. Sometimes additional reports, such as a facilities report, have been directed. A facilities report provides a much more in-depth analysis of what might be available to the patient in the community, with particular reference to specialist accommodation. In Community Treatment Order hearings there will not be a nursing report because the patient will be in the community and not detained in hospital.

The Tribunal Office is usually on top of chasing and sending out the reports to those involved in the hearing. However, it is important to keep an eye on what has been received from the Tribunal Office and with a hearing date looming, to chase them up if necessary. In s.2 cases, it is not unusual for reports to be received very last minute, sometimes within a couple of hours of the hearing, occasionally even less. If reports are not received in good time, then the Tribunal Office should send out directions requiring that reports be filed by a certain date. If this is not done then the Tribunal Office might be able to issue a summons, albeit enforcement is very difficult.

Ideally the medical report should be drafted (or signed off) by the Responsible Clinician, or a treating clinician who knows the patient well. Equally, the author of the nursing report should be someone who has had a degree of involvement in the patient's care. The social circumstances report is likely to be most useful when a patient has a long history of involvement with mental health services, or has been detained in hospital for some time. For a first admission under s.2, the social circumstances report is likely to have been drafted by someone who has never met the patient.

Reports should contain a summary of the patient's involvement with mental health services; any forensic (criminal) history; the circumstances that led to the current admission; the diagnosis or working diagnosis; their current presentation and treatment, and the author's recommendation to the panel. The reports should also identify the relevant statutory criteria and clearly set out the basis upon which each aspect is relied upon, for example identifying incidents or behaviours that meet the risk factors.

The medical report is likely to contain abbreviations and medical terminology that might not be easily accessible to someone without a medical background. It is worth considering purchasing a medical dictionary to help translate parts of the reports that are unclear because it is crucial that the legal representative has a full understanding of the evidence. It is also sensible to become familiar with the most common drug names (as well as their brand names) and what they are used to treat, along with their potential side effects.

The reports should also highlight any issues that might affect the patient's understanding of, or ability to participate in the hearing, and any adjustments that might help in this respect. This is useful for a legal representative to pre-empt any difficulties the patient might have with the hearing process.

Often, the reports are lacking in detail and contain inconsistencies. A legal representative should highlight these deficiencies in the questioning of the attending professionals, reminding themselves that it is for the Responsible Authority to prove its case, and raise any unresolved inconsistencies with the panel in their closing submissions.

Instructing an Independent Expert

Careful consideration should be given to any decision to instruct an independent expert and what it would add to the case. An independent expert could include a psychiatrist with a particular specialism, a psychologist, or an independent social worker, depending on the particular circumstances of the case. Consider that any expert will need to be more qualified than the Responsible Clinician, or more specialised, if the panel is to prefer their evidence over that of the Responsible Authority's.

Thought will need to be given to what issues the expert should address in their report and once received, it will need to be discussed with the patient. It will be down to the patient to decide whether or not the report is disclosed, as the legal representative must act on instructions. A draft report can be amended prior to disclosure if it is considered that something could be worded better or more clearly. This should be raised with the expert with a request for the change to be made.

A panel is unlikely to accept the written evidence of an expert who does not attend the hearing to be questioned. It is therefore sensible to make sure that the expert is available for any forthcoming hearing. Apply for a postponement if it is considered that their evidence is vital to the patient's appeal and the expert is not available to attend on the date listed.

Other Documents

The Mental Health Act Administrator of the relevant Responsible Authority or hospital in which the patient is detained should provide a document called the Statement of Information. This is a useful summary of the patient's history with mental health services and should set out the dates of any previous sections under the Act, as well as any discharges, renewals, and recalls from CTO. It should also provide the name of the Responsible Clinician, Care Coordinator and Nearest Relative, as well as other significant information including which authority is responsible for the patient's s.117 aftercare. This document can prove useful in confirming the history, or otherwise, as set out in the statutory reports.

Other documents that could be received are section papers and the AMHP report; as well as previous directions from the Tribunal Office.

Restricted Information

Rule 32 of the Tribunal Procedure Rules says that when the Mental Health Tribunal receives a document from a party, it must send a copy of that document to all other parties. Occasionally, a professional providing a report, or another individual such as a relative, might be concerned about some of the information within the report becoming known to the patient.

Rule 14 of the Rules provides that the Mental Health Tribunal can withhold certain information from the patient in very limited circumstances. The concerned author should apply to the Mental Health Tribunal with details of the information in question (in a separate document marked 'NOT TO BE DISCLOSED WITHOUT THE EXPRESS PERMISSION OF THE TRIBUNAL'), as well as the reasons why it should be withheld. The difficulty is how such a request conflicts with the patient's right to a fair hearing; a right enshrined in the ECHR. As a result, the threshold for withholding information is set very high.

As such, the requirements of Rule 14(2) are as follows:

> *The Tribunal may give a direction prohibiting the disclosure of a document or information to a person if—*
>
> *(a) the Tribunal is satisfied that such disclosure would be likely to cause that person or some other person serious harm; and*
>
> *(b) the Tribunal is satisfied, having regard to the interests of justice, that it is proportionate to give such a direction.*

Rule 14 was discussed in **RM v St Andrew's Healthcare** [**2010**] in which it was decided that when considering the 'interests of justice', the key test to be applied is whether or not non-disclosure of the document or information would allow the patient to make an effective challenge to their detention. In that particular case, the patient was being covertly medicated and without knowing that information he would be unable to properly challenge his detention.

Serious harm can be psychological harm as well as physical harm, albeit a real risk of physical retaliation would certainly be sufficient. The likelihood of an important relationship being seriously damaged is the most cited reason in an application for the restriction of information.

Legal representatives should be provided with the information, upon undertaking not to disclose it to the patient, and then, if so minded, file arguments with the Mental Health Tribunal (or with the Responsible Authority, if the matter can be resolved between the parties without a need to resort to the Mental Health Tribunal) arguing for disclosure. Arguments against withholding the information, in addition to it preventing a fair hearing without the patient being aware of it, can also be that the information has already been disclosed elsewhere. It is not at all unusual to find that a report that has already been provided contains the very same information. The application can be dealt with on paper prior to the hearing date, or might be dealt with by the panel on the day of the hearing as a preliminary issue. Often the parties can resolve between themselves that in fact, the information is not essential to the issues that the panel has to decide in any event, and so it can simply be placed to one side. Careful consideration should be given to this rather than burdening the Mental Health Tribunal with an unnecessary application.

SUMMARY

- The statutory reports from the Responsible Authority usually comprise a medical report, a nursing report and a social circumstances report and form a significant part of the evidence that the tribunal will consider.

- The reports may need to be chased up and the legal representative should diarise this.

- It is open to a patient to instruct an independent expert but careful consideration should be given to what this will add to the evidence.

- If an independent expert is instructed then they should be suitably qualified and have a particular specialism that will make their evidence persuasive to the panel. They should be available to attend the hearing.

- Rule 14 of the Rules provides that the tribunal can withhold certain information from the patient in very limited circumstances. The threshold is very high and the tribunal will need to be satisfied that disclosing the information would likely cause serious harm.

CHAPTER SEVEN

THE APPLICATION OF THE STATUTORY CRITERIA BY THE MENTAL HEALTH TRIBUNAL PANEL

Introduction

The Mental Health Act 1983 'statutory criteria' are the bedrock of the Mental Health Tribunal process. It is vital that the legal representative (and the panel) has this at the forefront of their mind throughout the appeal process, and particularly during the hearing itself. The panel's role is to apply the evidence to the statutory criteria and decide whether or not the criteria are met. It is also vital to bear in mind that it is whether the criteria are met on the day of the hearing, not, for example, on the day the patient was sectioned, or even 48 or 24 hours before the hearing. If the criteria are not met on the day of the hearing, then the panel must discharge the patient from their section.

It is the Responsible Authority's burden of proof. That is to say, it is for the Responsible Authority to prove that the criteria are met, and not for the patient to prove that it is not.

Legal representatives should avoid veering into advocating for or challenging particular types of medication or treatment for the patient during the hearing. A tribunal hearing is not the appropriate venue for such discussions and although a patient may put pressure on their representative to make various points of this nature, the legal representative must have in mind their duty to assist the panel in making the decision they are there to make, and that is whether or not the statutory criteria are met and therefore whether or not the patient should be discharged from their section.

Although the criteria broadly reflect the criteria for detention applied in the sectioning process as set out in a previous chapter, it is vital that a legal representative consider how the criteria are applied by a Mental Health Tribunal panel, factoring in the crucial difference that a patient in a hospital setting applying for discharge, is in a very different position to a person being detained and brought into hospital. The panel must consider the likely consequences of discharge and this is inevitably the premise behind many of the questions that the panel members will ask of the witnesses, as well as of the patient.

The Key Principles

Mental Disorder

The definition of what amounts to a mental disorder is extraordinarily wide and is defined by section 1(2) Mental Health Act 1983 as *"Any disorder or disability of the mind"*. Given this broad definition, there are very few cases that fall at the first hurdle of establishing the presence of a mental disorder. The most likely situation where this might happen would be a patient detained under s.2 with no prior history or involvement with mental health services.

A key exclusion is alcohol and drug dependence (s.1(3)). However, bear in mind that the alcohol or drug use in and of itself might have given rise to a recognised mental disorder, or the patient may have an additional comorbid mental disorder.

This aspect of the various criteria is the most likely to be conceded. Representatives will know that the definition is so wide that it is not worth troubling the panel with arguments over it, with time far better spent challenging other parts of the criteria.

Some of the most commonly encountered mental disorders are schizophrenia; mood-related affective disorders such as bipolar; dementia; eating disorders; psychotic disorders caused by psychoactive drug use; personality disorders; learning disabilities, and autistic spectrum disorder.

Learning disabilities

Section 1(4) defines a learning disability as *"a state of arrested or incomplete development of the mind which includes significant impairment of intelligence and social functioning"*. It is vital to note that under s.1(2A) of the Act, a learning disability does not fall within the definition of a mental disorder for the purpose of the longer-term sectioning powers unless it is also *"associated with abnormally aggressive or seriously irresponsible conduct"*.

Nature

The expression of the nature of a mental disorder is arguably more nuanced than the degree (below). When invited to describe nature, clinicians often fall into the trap of describing the nature of the particular mental disorder, rather than the nature of the mental disorder in the particular patient. The nature of the mental disorder in the patient is the course that the disorder has taken over time: for example, has it responded to treatment, or is it treatment resistant? Does it relapse and then remit? Do relapses happen rapidly or more gradually? Is it going to be life-long and enduring? Is the presentation complicated by illicit substance use?

In a patient detained under s.2 for the first time, it is unlikely that nature will be made out simply because there is no recorded history to look back on. Legal representatives should be wary of a clinician relying on nature in such a situation and direct their questions accordingly.

Degree

The degree of a mental disorder means its presentation at that current time. There will be a focus on symptoms that the patient has exhibited, usually within the few days to a week prior to the hearing date. Relevant questions that go to degree include: are they actively paranoid or expressing paranoid delusions? Is the patient responding to unseen stimuli (things that are not there)? Are they thought disordered? Are they difficult to interrupt or do they go off on unrelated tangents in conversation? Do they laugh inappropriately or incongruently? Are they displaying unprovoked aggression? Recent incidents of violent behaviour might also be relevant.

The tricky issue of insight

Many panels discuss insight in the context of assessing the current degree of the patient's mental disorder. It is also often considered as forming part of the nature of the patient's disorder. Insight simply means the patient's own understanding of their mental disorder, and their understanding of the impact that the symptoms of their mental disorder have on their own behaviours and on those around them. It can extend to their understanding of their need for medication. It is undoubtedly a tricky and somewhat abstract concept, and definitions can vary as a result. It is important to note that the concept of insight does not exist within the legal test in s.72 and in fact appears nowhere within the Mental Health Act 1983. There is no reference within the Codes of Practice. It can be controversial because if a patient challenges any aspect of the criteria, then it can also be said that they lack insight by virtue of the very fact that they appear to therefore not accept the treating team's views.

It is certainly open to a legal representative to challenge the professionals over the use of insight as part of any test that should be applied by the panel. It is worth bearing in mind however that discussions around and the inclusion of insight within the panel's consideration is arguably so ingrained that a legal representative would probably raise eyebrows if they sought to seriously challenge its relevance. What a representative can and should do however, particularly in cases where the history suggests that the patient has never really gained insight into their mental disorder, even when well, is to ask whether the treating team considers it a prerequisite to discharge and what happens if the patient never gains sufficient insight to the team's satisfaction.

The risk factors

In addition to there being a mental disorder and that mental disorder being either serious enough in its current presentation or over time, there must also be an element of risk to the patient, or to others. It is fair to say that the risk criteria are probably the most important factors in the minds of the panel on the day of the hearing, albeit all aspects of the statutory criteria are equal in weight. The majority of a legal representative's questioning, depending on the particular facts of the case, would be well spent focussing on how any perceived risks could be managed effectively in the community.

The risks in question must be connected to the patient's mental disorder (**R (on the Application of Li) v MHRT** [2004]). This is another line of questioning that a legal representative should consider. Can it be said that, in fact, the patient's gambling is simply a lifestyle choice, evidenced by a history dating back to before their mental health issues manifested, rather than a symptom of mania linked to their bipolar disorder?

Unsurprisingly, the risks associated with a particular mental disorder are hard to assess with any degree of certainty. As is often said, the best evidence is what has happened in the past, and the panel will hear about previous incidents and behaviours. The panel will want to be satisfied firstly that any alleged incident in fact happened, and they will assess the evidence on a balance of probabilities. Legal representatives should highlight any deficiencies in the evidence in this respect. The panel will then look at when and why the incident occurred. Was it too long ago to be relevant? Were there any mitigating factors? Was the patient provoked and their reaction within the spectrum of how any normal person might have reacted?

Health

The primary consideration here will be whether or not the patient will continue to take their medication if discharged from hospital. If the evidence demonstrates that this is unlikely, then the panel may find that this will lead to a deterioration in the patient's mental health. It is not only physical health that is relevant here, but mental health also. Evidence that the panel will consider will include previous admissions to hospital and whether or not these were as a result of a relapse caused by non-compliance with medication; whether or not the patient has complied, or complied under protest, with medication in hospital; has the patient repeatedly asked for doses to be lowered or complained about side effects that cannot be reasonably associated to the medication; have they told professionals that they are only taking it to get discharged from hospital; have they secreted tablets; has medication needed to be administered intra-muscularly (IM) because they have refused it in tablet form? Of course, the patient's own evidence, if they choose to give evidence, will be considered also.

Other factors that might be relevant to the patient's risk to health include neglect of physical health needs and the likelihood that they will take associated medication.

Safety

Risks to safety can be surprisingly broad; ranging from the risk of self-harm and suicide, to risk of retaliatory behaviour by others in response to, say, sexually disinhibited conduct.

Self-harm is likely to be a primary consideration if there is evidence of such behaviour historically. The panel will pay close attention to when the incidents occurred and how serious they were. Were genuine suicide attempts made which were only thwarted by intervention, or is the self-harm limited to some scratching of the arms with their own nails?

Although it might feel that the risk of self-neglect would be better dealt with as a risk to health, it is generally accepted that this falls under the heading of risk to safety. This is an area that treating professionals can be extraordinarily vague about in their reports and evidence, citing simply "self-neglect" with no elaboration or detail. This is insufficient. Has the patient simply lost a little weight through not attending to their diet correctly, or are they defecating in their own clothes having not bathed for a month? A legal representative should highlight where the detail is lacking and suggest to the panel that they need to be satisfied that the self-neglect is such that it presents a real risk to the patient's safety.

Self-neglect can also encompass the environment in which the patient lives, and covers, for example, hoarding behaviours, leaving the gas on or interfering with the gas supply, and poor food hygiene standards. The fire risks and other risks associated with such behaviours are obvious.

Some mental disorders lead to behaviours such as deliberate fire-setting. Driving when unfit to do so can also be a relevant risk factor.

Professionals often purport to rely on the risk of retaliation with very little, if any, evidence that retaliation has happened previously. Legal representatives should push the witnesses to be clear as to whether they are relying on actual previous evidence, or if the assertion is purely speculative.

Patients can often place themselves in vulnerable situations, for example exposing themselves to exploitation as a result of their drug misuse. Some patients become sexually disinhibited or go into public spaces undressed. It will take little effort to persuade a panel that such behaviours place the patient in a vulnerable position.

Risk to others

At first glance, this might appear to be the easier aspect of the risk factors. Indeed, a history of violence and aggression towards others, supported by a raft of criminal convictions, will certainly be difficult for a legal representative to shy away from. How historical the offences are, however, is likely to be relevant.

It is not just physical risk to others which is considered, but also psychological risk. This can include the harm caused to children within the household witnessing the patient's symptoms and behaviours, or the risk of psychological harm caused by sexually inappropriate conduct.

Other relevant risks can be driving when in a manic state; fire-setting behaviours; interfering with gas or electricity supplies when the patient lives in a block of flats; publishing harmful content online about other people, or sending threatening letters.

The availability of appropriate medical treatment

The requirement for there to be 'appropriate medical treatment' forms part of the statutory criteria for longer-term sections.

The definition of 'appropriate medical treatment' is not limited to medication; it can include psychological intervention, rehabilitation and nursing care (s.145(1) and 145(4)). Due to the broad nature of the definition, it is rare that this aspect of the criteria is challenged. There is no requirement for the patient to be actively accepting of the treatment, simply that it is 'available' and that the patient is not simply being held in hospital.

The panel medical member will often like to ask questions of the clinician about the treatment plan but there is no requirement for the treatment to be optimal or for the treatment team to demonstrate that it will achieve the desired outcome.

Admission under s.2 (s.72(1)(a))

The purpose of detention under s.2 is primarily for assessment, and so the requirement for there to be appropriate treatment available is not included. The criteria are therefore as follows:

> *(a) the Tribunal shall direct the discharge of a patient liable to be detained under section 2 above if it is not satisfied;*
>
> > *(i) that he is then suffering from mental disorder or from mental disorder of a nature or degree which warrants his detention in a hospital for assessment (or for assessment followed by medical treatment) for at least a limited period; or*
> >
> > *(ii) that his detention as aforesaid is justified in the interests of his own health or safety or with a view to the protection of other persons.*

As can be seen, the Responsible Authority has to prove, on a balance of probabilities, that the patient has a mental disorder, of a nature or degree (note it only has to prove nature *or* degree), and that detention is justified due to the risks to their own health or safety, or to others (again, note that the risk factors are in the alternative).

The use of the term 'justified' in paragraph (ii) suggests a lower threshold than for other sections where detention should be 'necessary'. 'Justified' simply means that the Responsible Authority have evidenced a valid reason for detention arising from the risk factors.

Admission under s.3 (s.72(1)(b))

The applicable criteria, which also applies to unrestricted hospital orders, are as follows:

(b) the Tribunal shall direct the discharge of a patient liable to be detained otherwise than under section 2 above if it is not satisfied:

(i) that he is then suffering from mental disorder or from mental disorder of a nature or degree which makes it appropriate for him to be liable to be detained in a hospital for medical treatment; or

(ii) that it is necessary for the health or safety of the patient or for the protection of other persons that he should receive such treatment; or

(iia) that appropriate treatment is available to him.

There are a number of differences between the s.2 and s.3 criteria. Detention under s.3 is for treatment rather than assessment, hence the additional criteria that appropriate treatment be available. Also, the use of the term 'necessary' rather than 'justified' is generally accepted to be a slightly higher test; the use of 'necessary' suggests that there cannot be any other way of providing treatment and managing the risks for the patient. The use of the phrase 'liable to be detained' is because there are patients who are placed on long term s.17 leave and so this wording covers such situations.

If a Nearest Relative has sought discharge but has been 'barred' by the Responsible Clinician then the Nearest Relative is entitled to make their own application to the Mental Health Tribunal. In these circumstances, the Mental Health Tribunal must apply an additional criterion as follows:

(iii) in the case of an application by virtue of paragraph (g) of section 66(1) above, that the patient, if released, would be likely to act in a manner dangerous to other persons or to himself.

The test of 'dangerousness' is clearly a high threshold and even if all other aspects of the criteria are met, if the Responsible Authority cannot prove dangerousness, then the panel must discharge. The additional criterion makes it more difficult for the Responsible Authority to prove that the criteria are met. Paragraph 32.23 of the Code of Practice states:

> *"This question focuses on the probability of dangerous acts, such as causing serious physical injury or lasting psychological harm, not merely on the patient's general need for safety and others' general need for protection."*

s.17(A) Community Treatment Orders (s.72(1)(c))

The criteria to be applied in the case of Community Treatment Orders are broadly the same as for s.3 patients, save for one crucial addition: the necessity of the Responsible Clinician's power to recall the patient. This is undoubtedly the focus of most Mental Health Tribunal hearings involving patients subject to a CTO.

The criteria to be applied are as follows:

> *(c) the Tribunal shall direct the discharge of a community patient if it is not satisfied:*
>
> > *(i) that he is then suffering from mental disorder or mental disorder of a nature or degree which makes it appropriate for him to receive medical treatment; or*
> >
> > *(ii) that it is necessary for his health or safety or for the protection of other persons that he should receive such treatment; or*
> >
> > *(iii) that it is necessary that the Responsible Clinician should be able to exercise the power under section 17E(1) above to recall the patient to hospital; or*

(iv) that appropriate medical treatment is available for him.

Note that the wording 'liable to be detained' has been removed and this is simply because the patient is now in the community.

Power of Recall

Legal representatives would be wise to focus their questions on this aspect of the CTO criteria. The panel will want to be satisfied that the power to recall the patient is 'necessary', as per the criterion, rather than 'desirable', which is insufficient to meet the legal test. A good question for a legal representative to put to the Responsible Clinician is whether or not the ability to recall the patient is simply a desirable 'nice to have', rather than absolutely necessary in this particular case.

Factors which are relevant include whether the patient has historically relapsed very quickly such that re-assessment under s.2 or s.3 of the Mental Health Act 1983 would take too long, and the risks are such that the patient needs to be recalled promptly; the community team's views about whether or not the power of the Responsible Clinician to recall is what is in fact keeping the patient compliant with their medication regimen, or whether there is evidence in the records of long periods of compliance in the community without a CTO; and of course the patient's own views. It is not unusual for patients on CTOs to value the structure and framework that a CTO provides them with; some even expressly recognising that without the recall power, there is a risk that they may stop taking their medication.

Section 7 and 37 Guardianship (s.72(4))

As a result of the burden of proof being on the patient in such cases, the criteria are worded differently. Also, the terms 'nature' and 'degree' are replaced with 'welfare of the patient' which is far broader. There is no need for reference to medical treatment because Guardianship would not be appropriate if compliance with medication was crucial.

The applicable test is as follows:

> *(4) … the Tribunal may in any case direct that the patient be discharged and shall so direct if it is satisfied:*
>
> *(a) that he is not then suffering from mental disorder; or*
>
> *(b) that it is not necessary in the interests of the welfare of the patient, or for the protection of other persons, that the patient should remain under such Guardianship.*

Recommendations (s.72(3) **and** s.72(3A))

There are no legal criteria for the making of a recommendation except that any recommendation must be for the purpose of facilitating discharge on a future date. Statutory recommendations are limited to s.17 leave, transfer to a different hospital and transfer into Guardianship. Occasionally a panel might be erroneously asked to make a recommendation that the patient be placed onto a CTO. A panel cannot make such a recommendation and can only recommend that the Responsible Clinician *consider* making a CTO.

Restricted Patients

Section 37/41 (s.73)

The applicable criteria are the same as for s.3 with the following addition:

> *(b) the Tribunal is satisfied that it is not appropriate for the patient to remain liable to be recalled to hospital for further treatment.*

Therefore, if the s.3 criteria are not met then the panel must go on to consider whether a power to recall is appropriate once the patient leaves hospital. If it is satisfied that it is not appropriate, then it must grant an absolute discharge. Absolute discharges are rare due to the likely seriousness of the underlying offence(s) which resulted in the application of the restrictions in the first place. The Secretary of State also has the discretion to grant an absolute discharge but the use of such power is extremely rare. A patient for whom it is considered appropriate that they be liable to recall is then conditionally discharged.

Conditionally discharged patients (s.75)

A patient subject to a conditional discharge can apply to the Mental Health Tribunal after 12 months, either for a variation to the conditions or for an absolute discharge. The burden of proof is on the patient and the power of the Mental Health Tribunal is entirely discretionary. That is to say, there are no statutory criteria to be applied.

Case law has established a number of factors relevant to the decision and panels will expect a legal representative to deal with the following points as set out at paragraph 57 of the judgment in **R (on the application of SC) v MHRT and the Secretary of State for Health** [2005]:

> *"57. Accordingly the Tribunal when exercising these powers will need to consider such matters as the nature, gravity and circumstances of the patient's offence, the nature and gravity of his mental disorder, past, present and future, the risk and likelihood of the patient re-offending, the degree of harm to which the public may be exposed if he re-offends, the risk and likelihood of a recurrence or exacerbation of any mental disorder, and the risk and likelihood of his needing to be recalled in the future for further treatment in hospital. The Tribunal will also need to consider the nature of any conditions previously imposed, whether by the Tribunal or by the Secretary of State, under sections 42(2), 73(4)(b) or 73(5), the reasons why they*

were imposed and the extent to which it is desirable to continue, vary or add to them."

SUMMARY

- The panel's role is to apply the evidence to the statutory criteria and decide whether or not the criteria are met, on the day that the hearing takes place. The burden of proof is on the Responsible Authority to prove this.

- 'Mental disorder' is widely defined in the Act. A learning disability does not fall within the definition of a mental disorder for the purpose of the longer-term sectioning powers unless it is also *"associated with abnormally aggressive or seriously irresponsible conduct"*.

- The nature of the mental disorder is the course that the disorder has taken over time and its key features.

- The degree of the mental disorder is its presentation at the current time.

- The risks associated with the patient's mental disorder will be a key focus for the panel.

- There is no requirement for 'appropriate treatment' to be optimal or for the treatment team to demonstrate that it will achieve the desired outcome.

- If a Nearest Relative has sought discharge but has been 'barred' by the Responsible Clinician then they are entitled to make their own application to the tribunal which must apply an additional criterion of 'dangerousness'.

- In CTO cases, the power of recall must be necessary and not just desirable.

- For restricted patients, if the s.3 criteria are not met then the panel must go on to consider whether a power to recall is appropriate once the patient leaves hospital. It is rare that an absolute discharge is granted.

CHAPTER EIGHT

THE HEARING: PART I – ONLINE OR ATTENDED?

Introduction

The hearing of the appeal will usually be listed to last half a day, for a morning or an afternoon. Morning hearings commence at 10.30am and afternoon hearings at 2.15pm. In some cases, a full day might be deemed appropriate, and this is often where an interpreter is required. It can also be where a patient has particular needs that mean a longer hearing is necessary to accommodate a slower pace. For those hearings, the Tribunal Office tends to set down an 11am start time. It is important to check the times on the documents. If a legal representative feels that the hearing will need more than the usual half a day, then they should say so on the application or notify the Tribunal Office.

It is crucial to arrive in good time as there are often issues to deal with prior to the commencement time. If a panel has an afternoon hearing (and it should be assumed that it does), then it is worth bearing in mind that the medical member may also have to fit in a pre-hearing examination for that patient after the morning hearing concludes. Punctuality, therefore, really is vital, and this is for both online and attended hearings.

Online v Attended

Prior to the Covid-19 pandemic, an online Mental Health Tribunal hearing was unheard of. However, in 2020, when the government lockdowns were implemented, it was vital that the hearing of appeals from those detained under the Mental Health Act 1983 continued to take place. With no visitors allowed into psychiatric hospitals for lengthy periods, the only option was to move the entire process online.

HMCTS began to implement 'remote' online video hearings using a platform called CVP (Court Video Platform), which was rolled out across all of the various courts and tribunals. Unsurprisingly, it was not without its teething problems with many judges and other court attendees finding out that they did not have working microphones or speakers, or worse still, that their laptops were too old for CVP to function at all. The equipment provided by the NHS to psychiatric hospitals up and down the country needed upgrading, and training provided to those who were going to be attending online Mental Health Tribunal hearings. During the latter half of 2020 and early 2021 there were many adjournments of hearings due to technological difficulties. This is now a far rarer occurrence, with attendees more aware of the sort of things that can go wrong, and how to resolve things when they do go wrong.

CVP hearings have enabled the Tribunal Office to provide panels for hearings far more easily, with panel members from all over the country often sitting together online. As there is no travelling involved, a panel hearing an appeal in Manchester in the morning, for example, can then hear an appeal from a patient based in Cornwall in the afternoon. This has made the whole process far more efficient with two hearings being able to be held in one day, whereas a panel might often be limited to hearing only one, depending on distances between hospitals.

The use of remote hearings has not been without criticism. Many legal representatives feel that patients do better with attended hearings, and that some judges are over-zealous with the mute function meaning that important comments from the patients are missed.

Patients are now given the option to elect for an attended hearing on the application form, and unofficial statistics suggest approximately 30% to 40% of hearings are being listed as attended.

Tips for attending a Mental Health Tribunal hearing on CVP:

- Make sure you have a working microphone, speakers and camera. You can test this via the settings on your device. You may have to invest in upgrading your equipment.

- Check your internet speed and quality of the Wi-Fi signal. You might need to upgrade to a better broadband package, and if signal strength is a problem, hardwire your device into the internet router rather than relying on the Wi-Fi.

- Consider purchasing a second screen. It is far easier to have the reports open on a separate screen and the CVP hearing on another, than it is to attempt to go between the two on a single screen. Make sure this is set up and working before the day of the hearing.

- Use a Chrome browser. This is the most reliable browser type for using CVP. Your device might not have Chrome installed on it so you may have to download it. Do this before the day of the hearing.

- Make sure all other video software (such as Zoom, MS Teams, Skype) is closed down. They can interfere with CVP if open at the same time.

- Make sure you are somewhere with little if any background noise. Video hearings seem to amplify irritating background sounds.

- Carefully copy and paste the link from the email provided by the Tribunal Office. Your device may automatically open a different type of browser if you simply click on the link, so open a Chrome browser and paste it directly into the address bar.

- Enter your name followed by your role in the hearing in brackets afterwards. This assists the panel in identifying who you are.

- Make a note of the guest pin code that would have been provided in the email from the Tribunal Office. If you have to leave the hearing then you will need the pin code to hand to re-join again quickly.

- Position yourself at the same level as your camera so that the panel do not see just the top of your head. Make sure there is no bright light source behind you as this can make you difficult to see on screen.

- For a morning hearing, connect to the CVP link no later than 10.15am, and by 2.00pm for an afternoon hearing. The Tribunal Office aims to allocate an online clerk to all CVP hearings who will let you into the CVP room and check your connection (resources mean this is not always possible). You may then be placed back in the 'waiting room' until everyone has joined, or alternatively you may be asked to turn off your camera and mute yourself.

- Be conscious of the mute facility. You will be invited to use it when not speaking and make sure you do. There is nothing more irritating for the panel than the sound of rustling papers. Equally, make sure you 'un-mute' yourself when speaking.

- You will be given a telephone number and pin code by the Tribunal Clerk. This is usually typed into the chat facility on the left side of the CVP screen. The number enables you to re-join the hearing by telephone if your video connection fails. If your internet goes down you might not be able to view the chat box when you need the number, so note the telephone number and pin code down on a piece of paper.

Attended Hearings

Attended hearings take place at the hospital in which the patient is detained. If the patient is subject to a CTO, then the patient will usually be invited to attend where the community team is located or another suitable location (this will also be the case for online hearings whereby the patient should be provided computer equipment to facilitate attendance, unless they are content to join from home).

If you need to meet with the patient prior to the hearing then this should be arranged with the hospital in good time. Depending on the patient, it might be possible to arrange to meet in the days prior to the hearing but sometimes this will have to take place immediately prior to the hearing itself. Bear in mind that the panel medical member might be undertaking a pre-hearing examination.

When visiting a hospital be aware that parking might be difficult, so allow additional time for this. It is not unusual to arrive at a hospital to find cars parked up on grass verges or on double-yellow lines. Often, a nearby residential street without parking restrictions will be the only option.

Psychiatric units can often have secure front doors with a buzzer or bell that you will have to ring to gain entry. Often, it will be one of the staff nurses that will need to come and let you in and this means there may be a lengthy wait for someone to appear. Be prepared to have to ring the bell a number of times before someone comes to the door.

Bring ID with you just in case the psychiatric unit requires you to prove who you are. Bear in mind that some units will not allow electronic devices for safety reasons so take a notepad and pen with you just in case. Bring printed copies of the statutory reports with you as a back-up.

The room in which the hearings are held will often be a re-purposed family room, or meeting room. It is not unheard of for Mental Health Tribunal hearings to be held in the ward dining area or even the kitchen. Some units are fortunate enough to have purpose-built tribunal rooms but these are few and far between. You should expect to be squeezed into a too small room, perched on a chair, with no table in front of you and your paperwork on your lap.

Paper hearings: Rule 35(E)

The only circumstances where a patient can opt for a paper hearing (that is when no one will attend and the panel will simply make a decision by looking at the reports and discussing it between them) is where a reference has been made under s.68 Mental Health Act 1983 for a patient in the community.

SUMMARY

- Hearings are usually listed for half a day, in the morning or afternoon.

- The patient has a choice of an online or in-person (attended) hearing.

- For online hearings the tribunal service uses CVP. Legal representatives should make sure they have compatible computer equipment and be aware of the idiosyncrasies of the CVP platform. Everything should be tested prior to the hearing date.

- Legal representatives should arrive for attended hearings in plenty of time. Parking is often difficult and access to the ward can take time.

- Attended hearings can often take place in a small re-purposed room with no table to lean on.

CHAPTER NINE

THE HEARING:
PART II – WHO ATTENDS?

Who attends the hearing?

In addition to the three-person panel (all three of which must attend or else the hearing cannot proceed), in attendance at an appeal hearing will usually be the legal representative and the patient, as well as the professionals on behalf of the Responsible Authority. These professionals (who in trial terminology are fulfilling the roles of 'witnesses') will be the Responsible Clinician, or a clinician attending on the Responsible Clinician's behalf; a nurse from the ward in which the patient is detained; and someone to speak to the social circumstances evidence, usually a social worker or Community Psychiatric Nurse (CPN) who may or may not be patient's allocated Care Coordinator. Despite it being described as 'preferable' within the Code of Practice, it is common for attendees not to be the authors of the submitted reports. They should however be familiar with the content of the report and be prepared to answer questions about the content.

Occasionally there are additional witnesses and attendees, such as the Nearest Relative or other family members, and trainee doctors or nurses who wish to observe only. Additional professionals can also attend if it is felt that their evidence might assist the panel. The judge should clarify who is who at the outset of the hearing.

Independent Mental Health Advocates (IMHAs) occasionally attend, in addition to the legal representative. The expectation is that they will provide support and guidance, rather than 'representation', and the Mental Health Tribunal has produced guidance to clarify the role of the IMHA. If a legal representative finds that an IMHA is also involved, having a discussion with them prior to the hearing is sensible, if only to ascertain whether they have any additional information that might prove useful. The panel will deal with the legal representative primarily, and then ask the IMHA if they have anything they wish to add.

Where it is the Nearest Relative who has brought the appeal, they are entitled to attend as a party to the proceedings. In all other cases they do not have an inherent right to attend.

Sometimes an interpreter will be required and this should have been prearranged and organised by the Tribunal Office.

Rule 38 (Rule 25 in Wales) gives the panel the power to exclude any person from the hearing if it considers that their presence would be disruptive, inhibit the evidence, or cause difficulty regarding an issue of non-disclosure. Witnesses may be brought in to give evidence but then be asked to leave again. The power to exclude any person extends to the patient themselves, however this is would be a highly unusual step and limited only to the most extreme of situations. Mental Health Tribunal panels should and will do everything they can to facilitate the patient's attendance in such circumstances and will be assisted by the legal representative's suggestions as to how they can move forward without having to remove the patient from the room.

Observers

There are a number of different types of observers that may be present at a Mental Health Tribunal hearing. In terms of those facilitated by the tribunal service itself, these are commonly appraisers and new tribunal panel members undertaking their induction observations. Although no permission is needed from the patient for this type of observation, if the presence of such person appears to be causing distress to the patient, and potentially preventing a fair hearing taking place, then the panel may terminate the observation and rearrange it.

The most common type of observation is trainee professionals such as junior doctors and student nurses. Applications to observe should be made to the Tribunal Office prior to the listed hearing date but it is common for the panel to be faced with an oral application on the day, or as is often the case, simply a statement from another professional that there is an observer present. The patient's views should be taken into account and the legal representative should make sure that this is done. If the patient is not happy with the presence of the observer, then the application should be refused.

Where do you sit?

Depending on the layout of the room, the chairs tend to be arranged in a straight line facing the panel. From left to right, if facing the panel, it is usually the person giving the medical evidence at the far end on the left, followed by the legal representative, then the patient, the nurse, and finally the person giving the social circumstances evidence at the far end on the right. The judge will sit in the middle of the panel, with the medical member to their right, and the specialist member to their left.

Rule 39 and non-attendance of the patient

Often, a patient will not want to attend the hearing. This could be due to feeling overwhelmed by the process, not wanting to sit through a couple of hours of listening to others talk about their mental disorder, or simply that they are content for their legal representative to deal with the hearing on their behalf. Sometimes patients are too unwell to attend.

Provided that the requirements of Rule 39 are complied with, then the hearing can proceed without the patient being present.

The legal representative should be prepared to deal with Rule 39 at the beginning of the hearing, if the patient has informed them that they do not wish to attend, or they are unable to attend, and the legal representative intends to invite the panel to proceed.

Rule 39 reads as follows:

> *(1) Subject to paragraph (2), if a party fails to attend a hearing the Tribunal may proceed with the hearing if the Tribunal -*
>
> > *(a) is satisfied that the party has been notified of the hearing or that reasonable steps have been taken to notify the party of the hearing; and*
> >
> > *(b) considers that it is in the interests of justice to proceed with the hearing.*
>
> *(2) The Tribunal may not proceed with a hearing in the absence of the patient unless -*
>
> > *(a) the requirements of rule 34 (medical examination of the patient) have been satisfied; and*
> >
> > *(b) the Tribunal is satisfied that -*
> >
> > > *(i) the patient has decided not to attend the hearing; or*
> > >
> > > *(ii) the patient is unable to attend the hearing for reasons of ill health.*

Representation

Patients who bring an appeal to the Mental Health Tribunal are entitled to be legally represented if they wish to be, with such representation funded by legal aid. To qualify for legal aid, representatives will need to be members of the Law Society's Mental Health Accreditation Scheme.

If a representative is appointed, the Tribunal Office will need to be sent written notification of their identity.

A patient can in fact appoint anyone to represent them, they do not have to be legally qualified. The only exclusions are persons who themselves are subject to the Mental Health Act 1983, or who are receiving treatment for a mental disorder in the same facility.

In most cases, a solicitor from a firm that specialises in mental health appeal matters will attend the hearing, but sometimes a barrister will be appointed by a firm of solicitors to attend on its behalf. Due to the limited funding available, most firms will prefer to keep attendance to the hearing 'in-house'. Where a firm has opted to appoint a barrister, or other external representative, as much information should be provided to the advocate, including notes of any previous discussions with the patient, and all of the statutory reports and any previous directions.

The standard of legal representation varies, as is the case across the broad sphere of legal representation in general.

There are three bases upon which a legal representative can act for a patient: the usual instructions-based representation by a representative of the patient's choice; under Rule 11(7)(a), which is on instructions, but by a representative appointed by the Tribunal Office; and under Rule 11(7)(b), which is on what is known as the 'best interests' basis, and is where the patient lacks capacity to appoint their own legal representative.

When a patient makes an application to appeal their section, the form provides the option for the patient to ask that a representative be appointed by the Tribunal Office under Rule 11(7)(a).

All legal representatives, no matter the basis of the appointment, should have met with, or at least spoken to, the patient prior to the appeal hearing. It is sometimes the case that a legal representative has not been able to get through to the ward by telephone, or the patient is in seclusion and not allowed to handle the telephone for safety reasons. If this is the case, and it is more likely to occur with remote hearings, the representative should inform the panel as soon as possible and request that contact be facilitated with assistance from one of the attending professionals from the Responsible Authority, or the Mental Health Act Administrator. It is best to avoid delaying the start of the hearing insofar as possible and so making this request promptly is advisable. A legal representative should be mindful that a pre-hearing examination might be taking place between the patient and the panel medical member immediately prior to the hearing. A panel should always allow time for a legal representative to speak with a patient if this has not been possible prior to the hearing.

The purpose of this meeting is for the legal representative to take instructions, or ascertain the patient's 'wishes and feeling' if it is a Rule 11(7)(b) appointment. They should discuss the evidence contained in the statutory reports; explain what the Mental Health Tribunal's powers are and how the hearing will work; who will be attending, and also to ascertain if the patient wishes to give evidence and if they do, at what point in the hearing they will want to do that.

Funding for Legal Representation

Patients are entitled to non-means-tested legal aid as part of the tribunal process, which is available for advice and representation from an accredited member of the Law Society's Mental Health Panel.

The intricacies of funding are too detailed and complex for the purpose of this practical guide but by way of a summary, Mental Health Tribunal cases are divided up into three stages: Stage 1 covers the initial advice, which includes a visit to see the patient and follow-up work. It also includes making the application. Stage 2 covers all the work up to the hearing; and Stage 3 covers representation at the hearing itself, and any application for a review or for permission to appeal. Funding is limited in amount which can place a great deal of pressure on the time that a firm can allocate to each patient's case. If the matter is particularly complex then additional funding can be requested.

Rule 11(7)(b)

Where a patient lacks capacity, a legal representative should be appointed to represent the patient under Rule 11(7)(b). Capacity in these circumstances is the capacity to appoint a representative. In assessing this, there is some overlap between the capacity to appoint a legal representative and the capacity to conduct the litigation without a legal representative.

The decision should ideally be taken prior to the hearing following the filing of an MH3 form by the Responsible Authority, but can also be made during the hearing, if the panel finds that the patient lacks capacity. Concerns about capacity are often flagged by the panel medical member as a result of a pre-hearing examination, or by the legal representative prior to the start of the hearing. The panel can then hear from the legal representative and from the Responsible Clinician, and decide whether or not to appoint the legal representative under Rule 11(7)(b). This will be dealt with as a preliminary issue.

Representatives who act under Rule 11(7)(b) must represent the patient on a 'best interests' basis: any application put forward at the hearing, or any challenge to any particular aspect of the statutory criteria, must reflect what would be best for the patient, taking into account all of the evidence. Unsurprisingly, this can often be remaining in hospital to be treated. Having met with the patient prior to the hearing and discussed the appeal and the information contained within the statutory reports, insofar as is possible with a patient who lacks capacity, the representative should ascertain the patient's 'wishes and feelings' – what the patient would like to happen insofar as the section and detention are concerned – and inform the tribunal of this. The patient's wishes and feelings are more often than not that they wish to be discharged from the section.

In practical terms, the legal representative will often begin by informing the panel that they act in the patient's best interests, that the patient's wish is to be discharged (if that is indeed the case), and that it is requested that all aspects of the statutory criteria are tested against the evidence. In closing submissions, the legal representative will say that having heard all of the evidence, it is accepted that the criteria are met and that whilst it is in the patient's best interests to remain under section, they wish to be discharged. A legal representative should not be frightened of making such a submission but a panel will understand that, with a patient in attendance, this is often difficult.

Adjournments caused by a lack of representation

A situation can sometimes arise whereby a patient has brought an appeal against their section and attends the hearing without any legal representation. A patient who has been assessed to have capacity is entitled to do this. There is no rule that states that a patient must be represented, simply that they are entitled to be so if they wish. It is prudent for any panel faced with this scenario to confirm that the patient does indeed have capacity by taking limited evidence from the Responsible Clinician, or attending clinician, on the point. They can also hear from the patient. If the panel hears evidence that leads it to conclude that the patient is likely to lack capacity, then the hearing should be adjourned for appointment of a representative under Rule 11(7)(b). A panel should direct that a formal capacity assessment be undertaken following the adjourned hearing, and the MH3 form filed.

A capacitous patient might attend a hearing unrepresented but then change their mind about being represented. In those circumstances, and provided the inevitable delay in not having the appeal heard that day is explained to the patient and the patient still wishes to adjourn, then the hearing should be adjourned to allow for the instruction of a legal representative under Rule 11(7)(a).

SUMMARY

- In addition to the three-person panel comprising the judge, medical member and specialist member, a number of other people will attend the hearing.
- For the Responsible Authority there is likely to the Responsible Clinician, a nurse and a social worker or CPN.
- The tribunal often receives requests for observers to attend but these requests should only be granted if their presence will not cause distress to the patient or interfere with the hearing.
- If the patient does not attend the hearing, then the requirements of Rule 39 will need to be met for the hearing to go ahead.
- Patients are entitled to legal representation and there is legal aid available for this.
- The patient can ask the tribunal to appoint a legal representative on their behalf under Rule 11(7)(a).
- If the patient lacks capacity to appoint a legal representative, then the tribunal should appoint a legal representative under Rule 11(7)(b) who must act in the patient's best interests.
- A patient who has capacity can opt not to be legally represented.

CHAPTER TEN

THE HEARING: PART III – THE PANEL & PRELIMINARY ISSUES

Panel Members and their Roles

The Judge

The judge's role is to chair the proceedings. They are required to ensure that the process is run fairly and that all the rules are followed. Provided that the overarching principle of fairness is satisfied, then there is flexibility as to how the hearing is dealt with. They will rely on the expertise of the two panel members and often leave the bulk of the questioning of the professionals to them, only asking additional questions if necessary. This will certainly be the case with the medical evidence.

It is the judge that is tasked with drafting the written decision following the hearing. As such, and given no recordings are made of the hearing, it is for the judge to take a clear and detailed note of the evidence during the hearing itself.

When referring to the judge, simply use the term 'judge'. Previously 'sir', or 'madam' or 'ma'am', were the expected form of address, but this was changed in December 2022 following a direction from the Lord Chief Justice and Senior President of Tribunals.

The Medical Member

The medical member's knowledge and experience is a vital tool to the judge and panel as a whole. They are often tasked with undertaking a pre-hearing examination of the patient, which is dealt with in detail below.

The medical member will ask the vast majority of the questions being put to the person giving the medical evidence on behalf of the Responsible Authority. This is because they have the medical knowledge that enables them to do this effectively and efficiently.

The medical member should be referred to as Dr Smith, for example, or as 'sir' or 'ma'am'.

The Specialist Member

The role of the specialist member is as it says on the tin; they provide an invaluable specialist insight into the vital community aspect of mental health care both pre- and post-discharge. They will have knowledge of the availability of mental health services; different types of accommodation available; how s.117 aftercare, or lack thereof, might be relevant to the particular patient; how safeguarding issues should be dealt with, and also how the involvement of mental health services impacts the family as a whole. The specialist member will ask questions of the professional giving the social circumstances evidence.

The specialist member should be referred to as Mr or Mrs Smith, for example, or as 'sir' or 'ma'am'.

Pre-Hearing Examinations

Often considered a somewhat unusual part of what is fundamentally a judicial process, a patient can elect to undergo a pre-hearing examination (PHE) by the panel medical member. This involves a meeting (either online or in-person, depending on the nature of the hearing) between the patient and the medical member during which the medical member will conduct a mental state examination of the patient and discuss the evidence contained within the statutory reports. The medical member should also have the opportunity to review the patient's notes.

In s.2 cases, in which a pre-hearing examination must take place, this should take place on the day of the hearing, and in all other cases it should take place prior to the day of the hearing. If the patient wishes to have a pre-hearing examination, then the request must be made 14 days prior to the hearing date itself (Rule 34(1)). Legal representatives should think about requesting a pre-hearing examination if the patient is doing particularly well or has improved since the drafting of the statutory reports, or if the patient might do better on a less pressured one-to-one basis rather than answering questions during the hearing itself.

Particularly with s.2 cases, legal representatives should be mindful that a pre-hearing examination might be taking place immediately prior to the hearing, and organise their time to speak with the patient accordingly.

If the patient is ultimately unwilling to engage with the medical member for the purpose of the pre-hearing examination, the duty on the medical member is to undertake the examination only so far as is 'practicable' and so if the patient suddenly refuses to participate, then the hearing can still go ahead. Equally, if there are other significant difficulties that arise on the morning of the hearing which makes the pre-hearing examination not practicable, then subject to submissions from the legal representative, the hearing can proceed. If the legal representative still considers that it would be in the patient's interest for the pre-hearing examination to take place, then they should ask for a brief adjournment to enable this. The panel will consider such an application in the interests of fairness as well as practicality and time pressures.

The medical member will then report their findings back to the judge and specialist member prior to the commencement of the hearing, and the findings discussed during the panel's pre-hearing meeting. The reporting back tends to involve a brief summary of anything of significance in the notes, such as recent violent incidents or refusals to take their medication; a description of the patient's physical presentation (were they unkempt and still wearing their bed clothes, or freshly showered and neatly presented?); a summary of what discussions took place and their responses to having the content of the statutory reports put to them; and then the medical member's view from a medical perspective: was there evidence of psychotic symptoms such as delusional beliefs or responding to unseen stimuli, or anything else that suggests the present degree of the mental disorder.

Sometimes a patient has taken a recent turn for the worse, or conversely is presenting eminently better than the statutory reports suggest. The process can also be very useful to the panel in finding out if the patient is likely to be attending the hearing and if they are, how they might need to be managed.

The pre-hearing examination forms part of the evidence which is what makes this aspect of the process unusual, in that the medical member's primary function is judicial in nature and yet they speak with the patient alone, with no legal representative present, report that back, and those findings can and do form part of the panel's decision-making process.

At the outset of the hearing, after the introductions, preliminaries and the legal representative setting out their client's position, either the judge or the medical member (usually the judge, but some medical members prefer to do so) will report back the findings of the pre-hearing examination to all present. If the judge is reporting back then they should check with the medical member that everything has been covered accurately. The legal representative should then be given an opportunity to clarify any aspect of the findings (note that this is strictly limited to clarification; a legal representative is not afforded the opportunity to question or cross-examine the medical member at any point).

Note the importance of the principle that medical members can only form a provisional view arising from the pre-hearing examination. Any suggestion in the feedback that a final opinion has been formed would give rise to an appeal.

The Tribunal Clerk

Some hospitals provide a clerk, or someone acting as a clerk, to assist the panel and those attending a Mental Health Tribunal hearing. Their role will be to assist the panel and other attendees by making sure they have copies of the reports, are taken to the right room, sat in the correct places and generally ensure that the hearing runs smoothly from a practical perspective.

If the hearing is online, then the clerk provided by the Tribunal Office will join the CVP link and check with the panel that they are ready to allow attendees into the virtual hearing room. They will check the video and sound quality of the attendees' connections and assist with resolving any issues that may arise. They will take a note of the names and roles of those who join so they can let the panel know who is online. They will also chase up anyone who has not joined as the start time approaches.

The clerk, whether in-person or online, can be a vital line of communication between the legal representative and the panel prior to the hearing commencing. If there are any important issues that the representative needs the panel to be made aware of, then the clerk is the best port of call to make sure these are communicated. Equally, the panel may use the clerk to convey important information to, or make enquiries of, the legal representative, such as whether the patient is attending the hearing or not. As with all staff working within the courts and tribunals service, they must be treated with the utmost politeness and respect, no matter the stressful circumstances a representative might find themselves in.

Preliminary Issues

Unlike court hearings, there is often a vast array of 'issues' that might arise on the day of a Mental Health Tribunal hearing that needs to be dealt with before the hearing proper can begin. This is due to the nature of the hearing itself and the very fact that at its heart is a patient who is potentially very unwell. These issues are often dealt with in a relatively informal and pragmatic manner, involving discussions with the panel about the best way forward. These discussions can involve just the panel and the legal representative, but can sometimes include the Responsible Clinician.

There may be conversations about how best to arrange the room and where attendees should sit, particularly if the patient poses a risk to others. Issues such as whether or not the patient will be attending, and if they are, if and when they will want to give evidence, are often dealt with prior to the start of the hearing. The panel is often greatly assisted by the input of the legal representative in dealing with pre-hearing issues that might arise, and the legal representative should be ready and willing to assist where able to do so.

Time will likely be spent making sure the panel has all the correct up to date reports and checking that the legal representative has them too, and has had an opportunity discuss them with the patient. It is not unusual for a legal representative to be concerned that, having spoken to the patient, the patient no longer has the capacity to instruct a legal representative and wants to raise this with the panel as a preliminary issue. The panel will then need to consider appointing the representative under Rule 11(7)(b).

It is also not unusual for a legal representative to inform the panel that they have not had a chance to speak to the patient yet, either because of practical difficulties on the ward, or because the patient has been placed in seclusion, gone AWOL from s.17 leave that morning, or is refusing to speak to them, or is too unwell. Letting the panel know at the earliest opportunity is crucial.

Withdrawals

The consent of the Mental Health Tribunal is needed for a patient to withdraw an application to appeal. References cannot be withdrawn. The Mental Health Tribunal must be satisfied that a review of the patient's detention is not required (**AMA v Greater Manchester West Mental Health NHS Foundation Trust** [2015]).

Requests to withdraw often occur on the day of the hearing. Once a withdrawal is accepted by the Tribunal Office or panel, the patient can then apply again, as the right to appeal has not been exercised. It is therefore often the case that a patient seeks to withdraw if having read the reports and received legal advice, they would rather save their right to appeal to a later date when they might have a better prospect of discharge.

A legal representative should make absolutely certain that a patient understands that if they withdraw then their detention will not be reviewed on that day. Careful consideration should be given to where the patient is within a particular period of detention and if withdrawing might mean they lose the right to appeal entirely within that specific period. Even where a representative considers that there is little prospect of discharge, it is sometimes useful for a patient to hear the treating team set out the reasons for that. Patients can often fluctuate in their wishes and feelings and a legal representative should bear this in mind.

Legal representatives may hear talk of 'tactical withdrawals', and the need for a panel to be satisfied that the request is not a ploy of some description, perhaps knowing that the patient is having a 'bad day' and being advised to withdraw. The reality is that a panel is unlikely to refuse consent to withdraw if such a request is made on the day of the hearing.

It is the patient's application after all, and although it can be frustrating for attending professionals who have prepared reports for the purpose of the hearing and taken time away from their work duties, the panel will recognise that it is the patient that should be able to decide whether or not to pursue the appeal.

Patients can apply to reinstate their application but only with the permission of the Mental Health Tribunal. This opportunity does not apply in Wales.

Adjournments

The Mental Health Tribunal wants to avoid adjournments if it possibly can. Avoidable adjournments are unfair to the patient by creating delays in having their appeal heard, meaning potentially longer in detention, and can also cause distress to a patient who has built themselves up to attend the hearing. Adjournments also present a logistical and resource problem to the tribunal service in having to re-list at short notice. A legal representative should therefore primarily work to assist the panel in reaching a solution to any difficulty that looks as if it is veering towards a potential adjournment.

There are of course, however, occasions where the hearing must be adjourned. This is when a fair and effective hearing cannot be achieved if the panel went ahead.

Sometimes, afternoon hearings are adjourned if the panel has a morning hearing that has run over. This is unfortunate and a panel will have done all it can to avoid this. This situation is far easier to resolve with an online hearing as a new panel can be quickly convened by the Tribunal Office. However, with an attended hearing it is highly likely that the afternoon appeal will need to be (potentially urgently) relisted. Legal representatives should be contactable in the lead up to hearing start times in case they need to be informed of any such changes.

Non-attendance of a professional

The interests of justice will rarely be served without the attendance of a witness such that they can be cross-examined on their evidence, if that evidence is to form part of the panel's decision, and it is disputed. It is a key tenet of our justice system that evidence be tested. As such, the non-attendance of one of the witnesses for the Responsible Authority will not be looked upon kindly. Non-attendance of someone to speak to the medical evidence will almost certainly lead to an adjournment of the hearing.

If any professional was aware that there was going to be a difficulty with them attending, then a postponement should have been sought. There is no guarantee however that a postponement will be granted, it will all depend on the circumstances and consideration of the overriding objective.

A panel may decide to proceed in the absence of a person to be questioned about the social circumstances evidence if, for example, the patient has very little, if any, previous involvement with mental health services and so such evidence is likely to be of minimal assistance in any event. There are however cases where the question of aftercare is likely to be crucial to the decision, and the panel can adjourn to obtain further information in these circumstances (**R (Ashworth Hospital Authority) v Mental Health Tribunal for West Midlands and Northwest Region** [2001]).

If it becomes apparent that there is key evidence that is required for the panel to come to a decision, then it is open to the panel to adjourn part way through the hearing such that someone who can give that evidence be directed to attend a relisted hearing. The panel should direct that the relisted hearing be listed before the same judge and members. This can be fraught with difficulties given the vast majority of panel members sit part time. Legal representatives should therefore carefully consider where the balance tips in terms of an application to adjourn; will the patient be better served by having their appeal concluded today, or is the delay vital to obtain crucial evidence that might realistically result in the patient's discharge.

Non-attendance of the patient

It is unfortunately not unusual for a patient to have gone AWOL during leave, or to be in seclusion on the day of the hearing. Whether or not an application to adjourn is appropriate in such circumstances will depend on a number of factors. Has the patient already provided instructions that they wish for the hearing to go ahead in their absence, or repeatedly made it clear to staff that they have no interest in it and would not be attending in any event? Or have they been talking about the hearing and looking forward to telling the tribunal how their detention is "illegal"? If they are in seclusion, they may be able to provide brief instructions over the telephone as to whether they want the hearing to proceed, or if absolutely necessary, through a member of the nursing staff (but bear in mind issues of legal privilege). The provisions of Rule 39 should be considered.

It is not unusual for a patient subject to a Community Treatment Order to not attend a hearing arising from a reference. In such circumstances, adjourning the hearing might not achieve anything at all and the next panel would be in the exact same position in a few weeks' time. The panel will want to be satisfied that the patient knew that the hearing was taking place that day, but chose not to attend.

SUMMARY

- The judge chairs the hearing and ensures that the correct procedures are followed and that the hearing is fair.

- The medical member will undertake the PHE and ask questions of the Responsible Clinician during the hearing.

- If a PHE takes place, this will happen prior to the hearing and the medical member will report back to the panel. The findings will be disclosed at the outset of the hearing. The PHE forms part of the evidence.

- The specialist member provides invaluable specialist knowledge on the community aspect of mental health care and will deal with the social circumstances evidence.

- There are often numerous preliminary issues for the panel to deal with including requests by the legal representative to be appointed under Rule 11(7)(b); requests for observers; and requests to withdraw the application, or to adjourn.

- The panel will do all it can to avoid adjournments unless there is no other option.

CHAPTER ELEVEN

THE HEARING: PART IV – ORAL EVIDENCE, SUBMISSIONS & THE DECISION

General Advocacy Tips

As with all good advocacy, the making of it is in the preparation. Going into the hearing knowing the patient, knowing what the patient wants, and knowing the reports, will put the legal representative in the best possible position to represent the patient effectively. Knowing which aspects of the criteria not to challenge, will make challenges to other parts of the criteria more persuasive. It can be said that a key skill of a good advocate is knowing what *not* to say, more than it is knowing what to say.

Being prepared to deal with any preliminary points that might arise competently and confidently, and then addressing the panel clearly and concisely on what the patient wants the panel to do, will not only instil confidence in the patient that they are in safe hands, but will instil confidence in the panel. A panel with confidence in a legal representative will listen far more closely to the submissions of that legal representative.

The Evidence

The burden of proof rests with the Responsible Authority to demonstrate that the criteria for detention are met, and the standard of proof is the civil standard: on the balance of probabilities, meaning that it is more likely than not, based on the evidence.

The evidence before the panel will consist of the statutory reports, the oral evidence from the professionals and also from the patient, and the findings of the pre-hearing examination, if one took place. The strict rules of evidence that apply in courts, do not apply to a Mental Health Tribunal hearing and so, for example, hearsay evidence is admissible. That is evidence that a witness has only heard about from someone else and is not in fact a witness to themselves. There is a lot of hearsay evidence in Mental Health Tribunal hearings: the content of the reports often arises from other professionals' notes and opinions.

The legal representative therefore is reliant on undermining the Responsible Authority's evidence, and, if it is of assistance, relying on the evidence from the pre-hearing examination, and the patient themselves.

A judge will likely ask whether the patient wishes to give evidence (they do not have to) and if so, if they want to do so before the witnesses for the Responsible Authority, or afterwards. A legal representative should be ready to answer this question at the beginning of the hearing and should carefully consider the patient's temperament in doing so. Most patients give their evidence first because there is often a risk that the patient will not be able to sit through the entire hearing and if they have opted to give evidence last, they may then miss the chance to do so if they have already left by that point. Commonly, a legal representative will say that the patient would prefer to give evidence first, but to then be given an opportunity to give some further evidence at the end if there is anything they wish to address or come back on. A panel will usually be entirely happy to agree to this.

Questions to ask the patient

Questioning of the patient needs to be approached in a carefully considered manner, depending on the patient and how unwell they are. Some patients can struggle to stay focussed, are hard to interrupt, and can often take the opportunity to air lengthy grievances about being detained and the NHS in general. They may have already answered questions during a pre-hearing examination and already had a discussion with the legal representative, and so feel they are being asked the same questions over and over. This can be both confusing and draining. A legal representative will not be criticised if they briefly address the patient before commencing their questions to recognise this and explain that the panel now needs to hear what they have to say, and if they want a break at any point, then they can say so.

The patient's legal representative will go first with the questions for the patient. The panel may have a few questions thereafter but these are generally very brief, if at all, and less likely if a pre-hearing examination has taken place.

Patients do not have to give evidence if they do not want to. Remember that the burden of proof is on the Responsible Authority and the patient does not have to prove anything. That being said, it is equally a patient's right to give evidence at the hearing, and it is often the patient's first opportunity to be 'heard' by anyone other than those treating them.

The following are examples of questions which might be appropriate to ask a patient in their evidence, but of course much will depend on the particular facts of the case and which parts of the criteria are being challenged.

- The doctor treating you says you have paranoid schizophrenia. Do you agree with this diagnosis?

- Do you think that you have any kind of mental disorder?

- Do you understand why people were concerned and worried about you?

- Can you tell us what happened just before you were brought into hospital?

- There is reference in the reports to an incident in which it is said that you were waving a screwdriver around and threatened to kill your neighbour. What happened?

- The reports say that you stopped taking your medication for three weeks before you were brought into hospital. Is this true? Why did you stop taking it?

- Do you think that stopping your medication might have caused you to have a relapse of your mental disorder?

- You told the panel doctor in the pre-hearing examination that you smoke cannabis as it helps relax you and keeps you calm. Some people think that smoking cannabis can make the symptoms of a mental disorder worse. Do you think that might apply to you?

- The reports mention that during some recent s.17 leave, you tried to abscond and now you have had your leave entitlement removed. What happened?

- Your family are very worried about you deliberately hurting yourself because there is some evidence that you have done so previously. What are your thoughts about harming yourself today?

- Can you tell us about the medication that the doctor has prescribed you?

- Has the medication that you have been given since coming into hospital made you feel better?

- If you were discharged from hospital today, would you continue to take your medication?

- If you were discharged from hospital today, would you engage with the community mental health team?

- If you were discharged from hospital today, would you agree to stay in hospital on a voluntary basis so that the team could continue treating you here?

- The social circumstances report says that unfortunately your previous accommodation provider has terminated your tenancy so you cannot live there anymore. Where would you go if you were discharged from hospital today?

Questions to ask the professionals

The panel will go first when it comes to asking questions of the attending professionals. This will usually involve them being asked to confirm the content of the report and whether there is anything important that has arisen since the report was signed. With the Responsible Clinician's evidence, they might be asked to briefly confirm which aspects of the statutory criteria they are relying on before the more detailed questions are then asked by the medical member. The specialist member will ask the bulk of the questions of the person giving the social circumstances evidence. Panels tend to share the nursing evidence questions between them, but all panels do things slightly differently.

Generally, the professional giving the medical evidence will go first, followed by the nurse, and then the social circumstances evidence, although there is no prescribed order.

Due to the legal representative going last in the running order in terms of asking questions of the professional witnesses, it is vital that they keep a note of what has been asked, so as not to repeat any questions unnecessarily. Of course, a legal representative can properly revisit a question if they wish to challenge an answer, or if they hope to elicit a different answer more favourable to the patient.

The bulk of the time is likely to be spent on the Responsible Clinician's evidence (or whoever attends to give the medical evidence), with a focus on the following (depending on the section being appealed):

- the history of the patient's mental disorder leading to the present detention;
- current presentation;
- insight;
- compliance and engagement, both historically and currently;
- what further assessments are awaited or still need to be done;
- current treatment and whether it is optimised or still under review;
- risk factors and any incidents that have happened on the ward;
- the likelihood of compliance with medication if discharged;
- what needs to happen before they would consider discharging the patient;
- for CTO patients: why the power of recall is necessary.

The questioning of the Responsible Clinician is likely to be the most important part of the hearing process. The panel will be keen to hear their evidence as the medical expert from the Responsible Authority. A robust medical member will certainly test the evidence but it will likely be left to the legal representative to really highlight and exploit any weaknesses.

The best approach to this is to focus on the relevant aspects of the criteria in turn. If it is a first admission, can they really rely on nature? If the patient has just given clear and cogent evidence which demonstrates a good level of insight, can it really be said that the degree warrants detention in hospital? If symptoms or evidence of risk factors are historical (even by a week or two), concentrate on forcing them to concede these. Put to them that any residual risks can be managed in the community and ask them to explain why this is not feasible given detention in hospital must be the least restrictive option for the patient. If the patient is subject to a CTO, and the Responsible Clinician has said that the power of recall will enable a quicker recall to hospital than a Mental Health Act 1983 assessment, highlight any occasions in the past when the patient has stopped their medication but stayed well for a lengthy period (do relapses really happen that rapidly?). If, despite treatment, the patient is still displaying evidence of delusional beliefs, the history might show that these delusions are and have always been treatment-resistant: how will the patient ever be well enough for discharge if so?

Of course, these are just examples of the lines of questioning that a legal representative might take. Much will turn on the particular patient and circumstances of the case but the key principle is to really focus on how the medical evidence can be challenged, not necessarily on a factual basis (although that can indeed sometimes be the case if the patient abjectly denies that an incident happened as alleged), but on how the facts, even if proven, do not meet the threshold for detention.

Questions of the nurse will tend to focus on the patient's current presentation, medication compliance and engagement, and risk factors as demonstrated by any incidents that have happened on the ward. Often, the nurse will have more of an up-to-date view of the patient's presentation and a legal representative might be able to expose weaknesses in the medical evidence if the Responsible Clinician's last review of the patient was, say, over a week prior to the hearing and the nurse is being far more generous to the patient in their evidence.

The witness giving the social circumstances evidence will usually go last, but this is not to say that the evidence is not of vital importance. Questions, led by the specialist member, will focus on discharge planning and what would happen if the panel were to discharge the patient. As such, the legal representative could, if appropriate, be suggesting to the witness that any proven risks could be effectively managed in the community and that the hospital environment is not the least restrictive option for the patient. Is there evidence that the patient has a robust support structure in place at home as demonstrated by the patient's husband, for example, being in regular contact with community mental health services and being completely on top of the patient's medication regimen? Again, it is a matter of highlighting that the evidence of the Responsible Authority fails to meet the threshold for detention.

Closing Submissions

The legal representative will be invited to make some closing remarks following the conclusion of the evidence. These should be brief. Unlike in a court hearing where the judge will fully expect a review of the key bits of evidence followed by arguments on the law, with reference to statutes and authorities, this is not the case in the Mental Health Tribunal and closing remarks should only take a few minutes in the vast majority of tribunal hearings.

The legal representative should briefly highlight any deficiencies In the evidence from the Responsible Authority, reminding the panel of the burden of proof, and focussing on the aspects of the statutory criteria that are disputed. A good legal representative will remind the panel of any evidence that shows that detention in hospital is not the least restrictive option for the patient and that they can be safely looked after in the community. Asking the judge if there is anything that they want addressed, or anything that has not been covered in the submissions, is a sensible way to conclude.

The Decision

After hearing all of the evidence and some final submissions from the legal representative, the panel will ask for some time to consider its decision. In all but the most complex of cases, this should not take long and you can expect to be invited back into the hearing room (or CVP room) after approximately ten to twenty minutes. There needs to be at least one person present from the Responsible Authority for the panel to be able to deliver a verbal decision in this way. It is unlikely that this would not be the case but if it is, then the decision will be emailed following the hearing.

Another reason why the decision might be emailed instead of delivered verbally would be if there is any concern about how the patient might react. Some judges will have already covered this in the preliminary stage with the legal representative or a member of the treating team, if the reports suggest a degree of volatility, but others might need prompting. If the legal representative is of the view that there is a risk to anyone present if the patient is told that they are not going to be discharged, then they should request that the decision be emailed.

The judge will not deliver a fully-reasoned decision at this stage, but simply inform those present whether or not they consider the applicable statutory criteria to be met and therefore whether or not the patient is to be discharged. If an application was made for a recommendation, then this will also be briefly dealt with verbally.

If the patient is to be discharged, it is good practice for the panel to email the Mental Health Act Administrator immediately following the hearing to advise them that this is what the panel has decided. A legal representative should remind the panel of this at the conclusion of the hearing in order to prevent any delays in the patient's discharge.

It is the judge's role to then write up a fully reasoned decision that deals with all aspects of the criteria, the evidence heard, the findings made, and the reasons for those findings. The legal representative will be sent a copy of the written decision by the Tribunal Office. It is expected that the decision will be received from the judge by the Tribunal Office within seven days of the hearing, or within three days for a s.2 appeal.

Appealing the decision

Not agreeing with the panel's decision is not enough to make it appealable; there has to have been an error of law, or serious procedural irregularity. There is an important distinction to be made between a 'finding of fact' and a misapplication of the law. 'Findings of fact' are decisions made by the panel about what it considers actually happened based on a weighing-up of the evidence, and bearing in mind the burden of proof. For example, the Responsible Clinician gave evidence that the patient assaulted a fellow patient, entirely unprovoked, on the morning of the hearing. Although the patient denied this, the panel made a finding of fact that the assault happened in the manner alleged, because it was also witnessed by the nurse who attended the hearing and supported the version of events. The Upper Tribunal, to whom appeals are made, will not interfere with findings of fact unless they are so irrational that no other panel could reasonable have reached the same decision, which, unsurprisingly, is extremely rare.

In England, the Mental Health Tribunal will first decide whether to review the decision and whether to grant permission to appeal. In Wales the application is only for permission to appeal.

Of course, the patient will need to agree to the appeal. The most likely outcome of a successful application to review is a rehearing, and so the patient will need to be sure that they wish to go through the process again. It may be that they have another right to appeal the section arising shortly, and would prefer to take that course rather than going through the appeal process.

The most common reason for appeal is that the decision provides inadequate reasons.

There is a period of 28 days to apply for permission to appeal once the parties receive the decision. This can be extended by application but there must be reason for the delay (Rule 5(3)(a)).

SUMMARY

- The key to good advocacy is thorough preparation.
- The patient has a choice whether to give evidence. If they opt to give evidence then they should be asked if they want to do so first, or after everyone else.
- The legal representative should carefully consider their questions to both the patient and the professionals, bearing in mind which parts of the criteria are being challenged.
- Focus on preparing a set of robust questions and challenges to the medical evidence as this will be important evidence to the panel.
- If the patient is seeking discharge, it is sensible to focus on how any risks are going to be effectively managed in the community.
- Closing submissions should be short and address the applicable criteria.
- The panel will usually give an oral decision at the end of the hearing simply stating whether or not the patient is to be discharged. Sometimes a decision will be emailed instead.
- Full written reasons are produced subsequently.

- There is a 28-day period to apply for permission to appeal once the written decision is received. There has to have been an error of law or a serious procedural irregularity.

CHAPTER TWELVE

THE MENTAL HEALTH BILL 2022

In 2018 there was an independent review of the Mental Health Act 1983, from which the 2022 draft Mental Health Bill ('the Bill') was published. At the time of writing, the Bill is still going through the scrutiny stage before it is formally introduced into Parliament to become law, and so there is still a likelihood that the draft will be changed before it becomes an Act.

In January 2023, the Joint Committee published its pre-legislative scrutiny report which made over 50 recommendations following receipt of 114 written submissions and over 100 responses to its online survey.

The key principle put forward by the government is that the new Bill will seek to *"give people greater control over their treatment and help ensure they receive the dignity and respect they deserve"*. It is said that this will be achieved through a number of changes to the law, including the following:

Mental disorder

The proposed new law will be that 'civil' patients can no longer be detained only because they have a learning disability, or they are autistic. To be detained, patients must also have a different mental disorder. This is to avoid the situation where people with learning disabilities or autism are being detained for long periods with little or no therapeutic benefit.

The statutory criteria

The Bill amends the civil provisions so that two tests must be satisfied before a person can be detained, or made subject to a CTO:

- Serious harm may be caused to the health or safety of the patient or of another person if the person is not detained or made subject to a CTO; and

- The decision maker must consider the nature, degree and likelihood of the harm and how soon it would occur.

Nominated Person

If a patient has capacity, then they can appoint a 'Nominated Person' which replaces the role of the Nearest Relative. An Approved Mental Health Practitioner will be able to appoint a Nominated Person on a patient's behalf. A Nominated Person will have all of the same rights as the current Nearest Relative, as well as a number of additional powers.

Period of detention for treatment

The Bill reduces the period that a patient can be detained for treatment from six months to three months.

Treatment

The Bill provides that there needs to be consideration of whether treatment is reasonably likely to provide a therapeutic benefit to a patient.

For certain patients, the Bill introduces care and treatment plans which should set out how the patient's current and future needs, relating to their mental disorder, will be met.

Community Treatment Orders

The Bill differentiates between a Responsible Clinician and a Community Clinician. The Community Clinician should be involved in decisions pertaining to any CTO, including the decision to implement one in the first place. There is to be mandatory oversight of the CTO by the Community Clinician, and any conditions should be made only when necessary.

Supervised discharge

Where a restricted patient is no longer benefitting from detention in hospital but the mental disorder is continuing, the Bill makes provision for lawful supervised discharge. The Secretary of State or the Mental Health Tribunal must be satisfied that the conditions are necessary to protect others, and that supervised discharge is at least as beneficial for the patient as detention in hospital.

Applications and References to the Mental Health Tribunal

The Bill proposes a number of changes to the time periods during which patients can make applications to appeal their section, and also to the frequency of referrals to the Mental Health Tribunal by hospital managers.

SUMMARY

- The Mental Health Bill 2022 is currently being debated in Parliament and, if it comes into force, will make a number of changes to the law.
- This will have a direct impact on how a panel deals with applications and references.

- Unless and until the law changes, the current law and procedure set out in this book applies.

MORE BOOKS BY LAW BRIEF PUBLISHING

A selection of our other titles available now:-

'A Practical Guide to Estate Administration and Crypto Assets' by Richard Marshall
'A Practical Guide to Managing GDPR Data Subject Access Requests – Second Edition' by Patrick O'Kane
'A Practical Guide to Parental Alienation in Private and Public Law Children Cases' by Sam King QC & Frankie Shama
'Contested Heritage – Removing Art from Land and Historic Buildings' by Richard Harwood QC, Catherine Dobson, David Sawtell
'The Limits of Separate Legal Personality: When Those Running a Company Can Be Held Personally Liable for Losses Caused to Third Parties Outside of the Company' by Dr Mike Wilkinson
'A Practical Guide to Transgender Law' by Robin Moira White & Nicola Newbegin
'Artificial Intelligence – The Practical Legal Issues (2nd Edition)' by John Buyers
'A Practical Guide to Residential Freehold Conveyancing' by Lorraine Richardson
'A Practical Guide to Pensions on Divorce for Lawyers' by Bryan Scant
'A Practical Guide to Challenging Sham Marriage Allegations in Immigration Law' by Priya Solanki
'A Practical Guide to Legal Rights in Scotland' by Sarah-Jane Macdonald
'A Practical Guide to New Build Conveyancing' by Paul Sams & Rebecca East
'A Practical Guide to Defending Barristers in Disciplinary Cases' by Marc Beaumont
'A Practical Guide to Inherited Wealth on Divorce' by Hayley Trim
'A Practical Guide to Practice Direction 12J and Domestic Abuse in Private Law Children Proceedings' by Rebecca Cross & Malvika Jaganmohan
'A Practical Guide to Confiscation and Restraint' by Narita Bahra QC, John Carl Townsend, David Winch
'A Practical Guide to the Law of Forests in Scotland' by Philip Buchan
'A Practical Guide to Health and Medical Cases in Immigration Law' by Rebecca Chapman & Miranda Butler

'A Practical Guide to Bad Character Evidence for Criminal Practitioners by Aparna Rao
'A Practical Guide to Extradition Law post-Brexit' by Myles Grandison et al
'A Practical Guide to Hoarding and Mental Health for Housing Lawyers' by Rachel Coyle
'A Practical Guide to Psychiatric Claims in Personal Injury – 2nd Edition' by Liam Ryan
'Stephens on Contractual Indemnities' by Richard Stephens
'A Practical Guide to the EU Succession Regulation' by Richard Frimston
'A Practical Guide to Solicitor and Client Costs – 2nd Edition' by Robin Dunne
'Constructive Dismissal – Practice Pointers and Principles' by Benjimin Burgher
'A Practical Guide to Religion and Belief Discrimination Claims in the Workplace' by Kashif Ali
'A Practical Guide to the Law of Medical Treatment Decisions' by Ben Troke
'Fundamental Dishonesty and QOCS in Personal Injury Proceedings: Law and Practice' by Jake Rowley
'A Practical Guide to the Law in Relation to School Exclusions' by Charlotte Hadfield & Alice de Coverley
'A Practical Guide to Divorce for the Silver Separators' by Karin Walker
'The Right to be Forgotten – The Law and Practical Issues' by Melissa Stock
'A Practical Guide to Planning Law and Rights of Way in National Parks, the Broads and AONBs' by James Maurici QC, James Neill et al
'A Practical Guide to Election Law' by Tom Tabori
'A Practical Guide to the Law in Relation to Surrogacy' by Andrew Powell
'A Practical Guide to Claims Arising from Fatal Accidents – 2nd Edition' by James Patience
'A Practical Guide to the Ownership of Employee Inventions – From Entitlement to Compensation' by James Tumbridge & Ashley Roughton
'A Practical Guide to Asbestos Claims' by Jonathan Owen & Gareth McAloon
'A Practical Guide to Stamp Duty Land Tax in England and Northern Ireland' by Suzanne O'Hara
'A Practical Guide to the Law of Farming Partnerships' by Philip Whitcomb
'Covid-19, Homeworking and the Law – The Essential Guide to Employment and GDPR Issues' by Forbes Solicitors
'Covid-19 and Criminal Law – The Essential Guide' by Ramya Nagesh

'Covid-19 and Family Law in England and Wales – The Essential Guide' by Safda Mahmood
'A Practical Guide to the Law of Unlawful Eviction and Harassment – 2nd Edition' by Stephanie Lovegrove
'Covid-19, Brexit and the Law of Commercial Leases – The Essential Guide' by Mark Shelton
'A Practical Guide to Costs in Personal Injury Claims – 2nd Edition' by Matthew Hoe
'A Practical Guide to the General Data Protection Regulation (GDPR) – 2nd Edition' by Keith Markham
'Ellis on Credit Hire – Sixth Edition' by Aidan Ellis & Tim Kevan
'A Practical Guide to Working with Litigants in Person and McKenzie Friends in Family Cases' by Stuart Barlow
'Protecting Unregistered Brands: A Practical Guide to the Law of Passing Off' by Lorna Brazell
'A Practical Guide to Secondary Liability and Joint Enterprise Post-Jogee' by Joanne Cecil & James Mehigan
'A Practical Guide to the Pre-Action RTA Claims Protocol for Personal Injury Lawyers' by Antonia Ford
'A Practical Guide to Neighbour Disputes and the Law' by Alexander Walsh
'A Practical Guide to Forfeiture of Leases' by Mark Shelton
'A Practical Guide to Coercive Control for Legal Practitioners and Victims' by Rachel Horman
'A Practical Guide to Rights Over Airspace and Subsoil' by Daniel Gatty
'Tackling Disclosure in the Criminal Courts – A Practitioner's Guide' by Narita Bahra QC & Don Ramble
'A Practical Guide to the Law of Driverless Cars – Second Edition' by Alex Glassbrook, Emma Northey & Scarlett Milligan
'A Practical Guide to TOLATA Claims' by Greg Williams
'A Practical Guide to Elderly Law – 2nd Edition' by Justin Patten
'A Practical Guide to Responding to Housing Disrepair and Unfitness Claims' by Iain Wightwick
'A Practical Guide to the Construction and Rectification of Wills and Trust Instruments' by Edward Hewitt
'A Practical Guide to the Law of Bullying and Harassment in the Workplace' by Philip Hyland

'How to Be a Freelance Solicitor: A Practical Guide to the SRA-Regulated Freelance Solicitor Model' by Paul Bennett
'A Practical Guide to Prison Injury Claims' by Malcolm Johnson
'A Practical Guide to the Small Claims Track - 2nd Edition' by Dominic Bright
'A Practical Guide to Advising Clients at the Police Station' by Colin Stephen McKeown-Beaumont
'A Practical Guide to Antisocial Behaviour Injunctions' by Iain Wightwick
'Practical Mediation: A Guide for Mediators, Advocates, Advisers, Lawyers, and Students in Civil, Commercial, Business, Property, Workplace, and Employment Cases' by Jonathan Dingle with John Sephton
'The Mini-Pupillage Workbook' by David Boyle
'A Practical Guide to Crofting Law' by Brian Inkster
'A Practical Guide to Spousal Maintenance' by Liz Cowell
'A Practical Guide to the Law of Domain Names and Cybersquatting' by Andrew Clemson
'A Practical Guide to the Law of Gender Pay Gap Reporting' by Harini Iyengar
'NHS Whistleblowing and the Law' by Joseph England
'Employment Law and the Gig Economy' by Nigel Mackay & Annie Powell
'A Practical Guide to Noise Induced Hearing Loss (NIHL) Claims' by Andrew Mckie, Ian Skeate, Gareth McAloon
'An Introduction to Beauty Negligence Claims – A Practical Guide for the Personal Injury Practitioner' by Greg Almond
'Intercompany Agreements for Transfer Pricing Compliance' by Paul Sutton
'Zen and the Art of Mediation' by Martin Plowman
'A Practical Guide to the SRA Principles, Individual and Law Firm Codes of Conduct 2019 – What Every Law Firm Needs to Know' by Paul Bennett
'A Practical Guide to Adoption for Family Lawyers' by Graham Pegg
'A Practical Guide to Industrial Disease Claims' by Andrew Mckie & Ian Skeate
'A Practical Guide to Redundancy' by Philip Hyland
'A Practical Guide to Vicarious Liability' by Mariel Irvine
'A Practical Guide to Applications for Landlord's Consent and Variation of Leases' by Mark Shelton
'A Practical Guide to Relief from Sanctions Post-Mitchell and Denton' by Peter Causton

'A Practical Guide to Equity Release for Advisors' by Paul Sams
'A Practical Guide to Financial Services Claims' by Chris Hegarty
'The Law of Houses in Multiple Occupation: A Practical Guide to HMO Proceedings' by Julian Hunt
'Occupiers, Highways and Defective Premises Claims: A Practical Guide Post-Jackson – 2nd Edition' by Andrew Mckie
'A Practical Guide to Financial Ombudsman Service Claims' by Adam Temple & Robert Scrivenor
'A Practical Guide to Advising Schools on Employment Law' by Jonathan Holden
'A Practical Guide to Running Housing Disrepair and Cavity Wall Claims: 2nd Edition' by Andrew Mckie & Ian Skeate
'A Practical Guide to Holiday Sickness Claims – 2nd Edition' by Andrew Mckie & Ian Skeate
'Arguments and Tactics for Personal Injury and Clinical Negligence Claims' by Dorian Williams
'A Practical Guide to Drone Law' by Rufus Ballaster, Andrew Firman, Eleanor Clot
'A Practical Guide to Compliance for Personal Injury Firms Working With Claims Management Companies' by Paul Bennett
'RTA Allegations of Fraud in a Post-Jackson Era: The Handbook – 2nd Edition' by Andrew Mckie
'RTA Personal Injury Claims: A Practical Guide Post-Jackson' by Andrew Mckie
'On Experts: CPR35 for Lawyers and Experts' by David Boyle
'An Introduction to Personal Injury Law' by David Boyle

These books and more are available to order online direct from the publisher at www.lawbriefpublishing.com, where you can also read free sample chapters. For any queries, contact us on 0844 587 2383 or mail@lawbriefpublishing.com.

Our books are also usually in stock at www.amazon.co.uk with free next day delivery for Prime members, and at good legal bookshops such as Wildy & Sons.

We are regularly launching new books in our series of practical day-to-day practitioners' guides. Visit our website and join our free newsletter to be kept informed and to receive special offers, free chapters, etc.

You can also follow us on Twitter at www.twitter.com/lawbriefpub.

www.ingramcontent.com/pod-product-compliance
Ingram Content Group UK Ltd.
Pitfield, Milton Keynes, MK11 3LW, UK
UKHW020148290926
15471UKWH00004B/750

9 781916 698123